Mind Control Hypnosis

By Dantalion Jones

Author of

Perfected Mind Control – The Unauthorized Black Book Of Hypnotic Mind Control

Mind Control 101 – How To Influence the Thoughts and Minds of Others Without Them Knowing or Caring

The Forbidden Book Of Getting What You Want

Cult Control – The Building of a Cult

The Delta Success Programming CD series

Mind Control Hypnosis

Mind Control Publishing

Copyright   Dantalion Jones 2010

ISBN 1448619181
EAN-13 9781448619184

All rights reserved. Without limiting the rights under copyrights reserved above, no part of this publication may be reproduced, stored in, or introduced into a retrieval system, or transmitted, in any form or by any means (electronic, mechanical, photocopying, recording, or otherwise), without the prior written permission of the copyright owner.

Formatted using Open Office

Dedication

To all those wonderful friends and brothers living "behind the veil" who have brought me from darkness to light and who taught me that there is no greater ambition than to cast a boulder into the current of time and alter the course of history. They have shown me the programs we live by and the programs behind the programs. They have shown me that while we all value free will very few truly have it ...or want it.

Also

To my faithful djinn, familiar and constant companion, Dantalion, the seventy-first spirit of the Goetia, "His Office is to teach all Arts and Sciences unto any; and to declare the Secret Counsel of any one; for he knoweth the Thoughts of all Men and Women, and can change them at his Will. He can cause Love, and show the Similitude of any person, and show the same by a Vision, let them be in what part of the World they Will."

Table of Contents

Note to Reader. 1
Introduction. 2
What is Mind Control?. 5
Hypnosis Myths Made True 7
What Is Hypnosis?. 8
Who Can and Cannot Be Hypnotized?. 16
Who NOT to Hypnotize. 18
Can People Be Made To Do Things Against Their Will?. . . . 20
The Myth of The Will. 20
Transference and Values Elicitation. 23
Values Elicitation. 24
Undressing in Public: An Example of Hypnosis. 30
Overview of The Hypnosis Process. 32
The Pre-Talk. 34
The Entrainment. 39
Using Reward and Punishment. 40
The Hypnotic Induction. 42
Five Things That Assist To Induce Hypnosis. 49
A Comment on Inductions. 52
Rapid Hypnotic Inductions 53
Subtle "Tricks" Within The Hypnosis Process. 57
Tips, Techniques, and Tricks of The Hypnotist. 65
Using The Subject's Own Words. 65
Pointing Out Successes and Using Them. 66
The Voice of Experience. 67
Places In The Mind 68
The Hypnotic Seal 78
Creating Useful Mental Structures In The Mind. 84
Training to Hallucinate. 85
Bottles, Boxes, Treasure Chests and Containers. 87
Useful Hypnosis Scripts. 96
The Mirror of The Future. 96
The Cravings Crusher. 100
Creating Negative Hallucinations. 104
The NLP Phobia Hypnosis Process. 107

For Fun: Hypnotic Drunkenness 111
The Dantalion Jones Hypnosis Setting. 114
The PMC Processes. 117
Conclusion. 187

Mind Control Hypnosis

Note to Reader

Traditional martial arts are filled with veteran fighters who have dedicated their lives to learn their craft. The most senior among them have gained such skill that they make their actions appear effortless. They may even have come to believe that if they can do it so easily that it must be easy for others. That clearly is not the case.

They have forgotten the years of work and training they have put into learning and mastery. They may even treat students and newcomers like idiots for not knowing what has taken them years to learn.

My experience has often left me cynical and jaded as if, at times, I've forgotten the seeds of learning. To those I hypnotize I forget they are sometimes afraid and anticipate something magical. To those I teach I tend to be impatient with their fear and timidity.

Here is my very best advice to the reader who wants to learn and practice hypnosis: be fearless. Go out and test what you've learned until you've mastered it. Don't wait to learn more when you have enough to act now. This is good advice in hypnosis and in life.

Any mistake you make by being bold and audacious can usually be overcome by greater audacity.

Perhaps this sounds foolhardy, but timidity will only yield you a life half lived.

Be Fearless.

Dantalion Jones

Mind Control Hypnosis

Introduction

As with most of the books I've written, I will attempt to exploit the reader's sincere and sometimes twisted interest in mind control and, in this case, specifically hypnosis.

For many there has long existed a romance with being able to talk someone into a lethargic and robotic state in which they will do things without any personal inhibition. The mind runs wild with possibilities. Many a child's juvenile fantasies for power and control have been fueled by witnessing a performing hypnotist at the county fair.

But theory and reality seldom come into a perfect convergence, and this holds true of hypnosis as well.

However, my many years of doing hypnosis in various settings helped prove to me several things that most hypnotists will work fervently to deny or to explain away as myth. I suspect this is because most hypnotists have never dedicated themselves to testing the limits of the hypnotic arts. They have likely been subjected to narrow minded training that indoctrinated them to work within rigid constraints, and therefore hold limited ideas of what's possible.

While it is wise to understand what these limits are, I've never found a benefit to blindly accepting them. The power of hypnosis is underrated because the power of the mind is underrated. The mind can decide to control its breathing, heart beat, blood pressure and other things that were once thought to be involuntary.

Studying, learning and practicing hypnosis and related skills like NLP have been passions for me and, were I to die today, I could say have played a major part in the "great work" of my life.

I'd like to point out that this book will talk specifically about the *authoritarian* style of hypnosis, as opposed to the *permissive* style of hypnosis made famous by Milton Erickson.

Authoritarian hypnosis is what people are used to seeing when they go to a hypnosis show, and is what they are most familiar with from TV and media. It is an overt style of hypnosis where the hypnotist and subject have both agreed upon their roles. The subject agrees from the onset to follow the hypnotist's suggestions, and the hypnotist agrees to keep the subject safe and offer good healthy suggestions.

Many people have made powerful claims about how someone can be covertly hypnotized to do things. Even I have written on this subject (see my book *Mind Control Language Patterns*.) Let me make it clear that this book has none of that. You'll be exposed to techniques and methodologies some would consider "sneaky," but none of it is covert.

And so in this book I intend to explain what I've learned doing hypnosis on people who know they are going to be hypnotized. A portion of this book is likely to be new, profane and even sacrilege. I make no apology if a few icons fall during these heresies. I seek only to tell what I've discovered. Let us not forget that Galileo and Charles Darwin were also heretics.

In this book I'll explain the theory and application of *my* experience in the art of hypnosis. This will include how hypnosis relates to the concept of mind control, and a sincere look at the so-called "myths" of hypnosis. It will uncover a shocking look at the concept of the human will, and a new but

Mind Control Hypnosis

meaningful definition of hypnosis. The details of the hypnotic experience will be described, beginning at the setting used for hypnosis, the preparation for hypnosis, and what to say. Lastly, you'll be given the specific hypnotic scripts that have been used to create positive and dramatic change in others.

For the neophyte this book is designed to inform. For the experienced hypnotist it may inform and also surprise.

Mind Control Hypnosis

What is Mind Control?

Story #1
A man enters an AA meeting for the first time. He has personally experienced what alcohol has done to him, his family and his job. He sees all the people one by one describing their battle with addiction. He feels as if this is his only hope for a better life. He stands and sees the eyes of others focus on him, his voice quivering, "Hello, my name is…"

Story #2
The doctor has told her what she has already suspected. She has CPD, cardiopulmonary disease. Her life long love affair with the cigarette will either have to end now, or she will have to begin carrying a bottle of oxygen wherever she goes. The thought of stopping smoking creates a shot of anxiety as she opens the paper and sees an advertisement that reads "Stop Smoking With Hypnosis is 20 Minutes."

Story #3
The young woman enters her appointment with her counselor weighed down by a lifetime of guilt. The secret that she has held all her life was now about to end. The words come out. Tears are shed. At the end of the session she notices a lightness in her step. Something has changed within her and she realized she can begin to make better choices in her life.

Let's make it clear. Mind control is happening all around us.

This is not the fearful mind control envisioned

Mind Control Hypnosis

by the paranoid conspiracy theorist who see covert signs and manipulations written on the back of a dollar bill. This is the mind control that happens within the settings we walk through every day. It is the mind control that happens in friendly conversations and the subtle pleas that tug at us in everyday life.

Is mind control good or bad?

Neither. Mind control is the sincere attempt to influence our thoughts to effect our lives in some measurable way. To look objectively at mind control we must abandon all the moralistic garbage others have given it.

Mind control is at the very core of our communication. Even when we talk to ourselves (and we do it more often than we might admit) we are doing it to influence ourselves.

People are even willing to employ the mind control skills of others when their own mind control skills fail. This is why people visit or hire psychologists, hypnotists, and coaches.

There often looms an aura of mystery around these people but still their services are needed and desired.

Hypnosis is probably the most mysterious and misunderstood form of mind control. There have been endless books written on the subject that often say much of the same thing. The authors of these books are usually experienced and well meaning professionals, but are invested in maintaining a divide between "mind control" and "hypnosis".

I intend to close that divide.

Hypnosis *is* a form of mind control. That does not make it bad. It makes it an extension of how we communicate. Nothing more.

Mind Control Hypnosis

Hypnosis Myths Made True
(Based on my long and jaded experience)

Like psychology, neuroscience ,or any field of the mind, it is hard to find anyone who can speak about hypnosis with any degree of thorough understanding. Those who can are usually people who have at least some training and, like psychologists and neurologists, are not likely to be present at every dinner party you go to.

The result is that our understanding is based on an imperfect knowledge, and we are left to rely on hearsay, fantasy and popular fiction to fill in the blanks. From this "half knowledge" comes myths and legends about hypnosis.

That we can call them myths gives most hypnotists the license to dispel them which allow their subjects to feel safe and secure.

But let us not forget that the word "myth" does not mean "false" or "lie." It means "story." We will review these stories, and while others may try to dispel them, we will explain and elaborate on them.

The two biggest myths to be explained are as follows:

- Some people cannot be hypnotized.

- You cannot make someone do something against their will by using hypnosis.

You may be a bit surprised.

Let's first look at what hypnosis is.

Mind Control Hypnosis

What Is Hypnosis?

Do a little research and you'll find that there are many people who have given different definitions of hypnosis. For the most part, these definitions are accurate and give a good idea of what constitutes hypnosis. Here are some of the definitions:

James Braid (June 19, 1795 – March 25, 1860)

The real origin and essence of the hypnotic condition is the induction of a habit of abstraction or mental concentration, in which, as in reverie or spontaneous abstraction, the powers of the mind are so much engrossed with a single idea or train of thought, as, for the nonce, to render the individual unconscious of, or indifferently conscious to, all other ideas, impressions, or trains of thought.

Hippolyte Bernheim (1840-1919)

To define hypnotism as induced sleep, is to give a too narrow meaning to the word, to overlook the many phenomena which suggestion can bring about independently of sleep. I define hypnotism as the induction of a peculiar psychical condition which increases the susceptibility to suggestion. Often, it is true, the sleep that may be induced facilitates suggestion, but it is not the necessary preliminary. It is suggestion that rules hypnotism.

I have tried to show that suggested sleep differs in no respect from natural sleep. The same phenomena of suggestion can be obtained in natural sleep, if one succeeds in putting one's self into relationship [rapport] with the sleeping person without waking him.

Mind Control Hypnosis

This new idea which I propose concerning the hypnotic influence, this wider definition given to the word hypnotism, permits us to include in the same class of phenomena all the various methods which, acting upon imagination, induce the psychical condition of exalted susceptibility to suggestion [hyper-suggestibility] with or without sleep.

Sigmund Freud (May 6, 1856 – September 23, 1939)

It has long been known, though it has only been established beyond all doubt during the last few decades, that it is possible, by certain gentle means, to put people into a quite peculiar mental state very similar to sleep and on that account described as 'hypnosis.' [...] The hypnotic state exhibits a great variety of gradations. In its lightest degree the hypnotic subject is aware only of something like a slight insensibility, while the most extreme degree, which is marked by special peculiarities, is known as 'somnambulism', on account of its resemblance to the natural phenomena of sleep-walking. But hypnosis is in no sense a sleep like our nocturnal sleep or like the sleep produced by drugs. Changes occur in it and mental functions are retained during it which are absent in normal sleep.

The UK Book of Statues

"Hypnotism" includes hypnotism, mesmerism and any similar act or process which produces or is intended to produce in any person any form of induced sleep or trance in which the susceptibility of the mind of that person to suggestion or direction is

increased or intended to be increased but does not include hypnotism, mesmerism or any similar act or process which is self-induced. [The Hypnotism Act, 1952]

The British Medical Association

A temporary condition of altered attention in the subject which may be induced by another person and in which a variety of phenomena may appear spontaneously or in response to verbal or other stimuli. These phenomena include alterations in consciousness and memory, increased susceptibility to suggestion, and the production in the subject of responses and ideas unfamiliar to him in his usual state of mind. Further, phenomena such as anaesthesia, paralysis and rigidity of muscles, and vasomotor changes can be produced and removed in the hypnotic state. [BMA, 'Medical use of Hypnotism', 1955]

Dave Elman (1900-1967)

Hypnosis is a state of mind in which the critical faculty of the human is bypassed, and selective thinking established.

Gil Boyne

Hypnosis is a natural state of mind with special identifying characteristics:

1. An extraordinary quality of relaxation.
2. An emotionalized desire to satisfy the suggested behaviour: The person feels like doing what the hypnotist suggests, provided that what is suggested does not generate conflict with his belief system.

3. The organism becomes self-regulating and produces normalization of the central nervous system.
4. Heightened and selective sensitivity to stimuli perceived by the five senses and four basic perceptions.
5. Immediate softening of psychic defenses.

The UK Council for Psychotherapy

Hypno-Psychotherapy originates in procedures and practices discovered and recorded over the last three hundred years. The first formal exploration and beneficial application of hypnotic phenomena began in the 1750's. Increasing awareness, over the last 100 years, of the pervasiveness and importance in human experience of what are now more appropriately described as 'altered state phenomena' has led to huge shifts in theoretical understanding, convergence with discoveries emerging from modern neuro-science and much increased consistency in application. This has been accompanied by the creation of a substantial scientific literature.

Hypnosis describes a range of naturally occurring states of altered awareness which may vary from momentary distractions and 'absences' through much enhanced states of relaxation to very deep states of inward focus and awareness.. The mental processes which can occur in any of these states, appropriately utilised, are generally far more flexible and potentially far more powerful in effecting change than those we can achieve in most everyday states of active conscious awareness. These states may be induced quite formally or quite naturalistically, in an almost unnoticeable way, depending on the requirement of the problem, the capability of the practitioner and the needs of the client.

As well as alleviating a range of disadvantageous habits and many physical ailments, Hypno-Psychotherapy also deals in deep-seated problems involving themes and procedures in many ways similar to those addressed by many other branches of Psychotherapy. Hypno-Psychotherapists take a wide-ranging and eclectic view in helping clients to understand and to alleviate psychological difficulties.

At one end of the spectrum Hypno-Psychotherapists base their diagnostic work and therapeutic strategies in modern information processing models whilst others have emphases in other orientations (e.g. Cognitive, Cognitive Analytic, Psychodynamic or Counselling modes). In all cases, practice differs from other forms of psychotherapy in the deliberate (direct and indirect) use of altered mental states and supporting therapeutic structures as the principal medium for effecting change.

It should be emphasized that the methods and strategies used in Hypno-Psychotherapy, though powerful and often speedy in effect, also respect and are attuned to the qualities and characteristics of the individual client involved. They seek to utilize and enhance the resources and capabilities that reside in all people, and do not by any means require the client to respond to any standardized technique or to fit into any standardized pattern.

While flexibility is paramount, the working relationship in Hypno-Psychotherapy strives for equality between client and therapist, in providing a safe and supportive environment, where the client can explore and clarify relevant personal matters. In encouraging agreed modification of the client's beliefs, emotional responses and behaviour, the problem may require the therapist to assume a more active or directive role. In shorter term engagements, it can be used to inculcate skills and overcome limiting habits or personal and social inhibitions. During longer-term therapy, the working relationship may present a dynamic context for the client to examine and work through important self-protection issues, including the reframing and resolution of challenging early experiences and liberation from previous blocks to personal development.

Hypno-Psychotherapy may be valuable to anyone seeking to resolve specific problems, or for personal development.

Whitney Hibbard and Raymond Worring

Hypnosis is a controlled dissociated state in which the conscious, critical, intellectual, and logical portion of one's mind is disassociated, inhibited, misdirected, or distracted, allowing for direct access to one's subconscious, thereby making the elicitation of natural and preexisting subconscious mental mechanisms possible.

Now that you have an idea of what others think hypnosis is and, if you have experienced hypnosis, these definitions can all seem accurate, for the most part.

Here is the Dantalion Jones definition of hypnosis:

Mind Control Hypnosis

Hypnosis is the exact following of suggestions in order to create a meaningful experience.

That's it. Short, simple and to the point.

Hypnosis is the exact following of suggestions in order to create a meaningful experience.

In looking at the parts of this definition we'll start with the word *suggestion.* A suggestion is just that, a suggestion. It is not an order, command or imperative. A suggestion does not have to be followed. At some level there must be an agreement by the hypnotic subject to follow the suggestions. This can be an overt or implied agreement, but without following the suggestions nothing can take place.

The next words to examine are *exact following.* Following suggestions exactly allows the hypnotist to describe in detail the experience the subject is to mentally enact. It allows the subject to feel emotions that are suggested, reactions and responses that are suggested, and to make possible things that at one time might not have been within the subject's realm of reality.

To create a meaningful experience are the remaining words. To understand why a *meaningful experience* is needed, consider that most people who want to make changes already know what they should do. Overweight people know that they should limit their food and increase their physical activity, but simply knowing the information does not make people change. On the other hand, when people go through experiences that are meaningful to them they can make dramatic and significant changes

Mind Control Hypnosis

immediately.

Consider people who have gone through the experience of a religious conversion. They have been known to change their behaviors in a major and dramatic way. The same is true when one has a life threatening experience.

In both experiences they reevaluate their life and behaviors and from that *meaningful experience* the information became important enough to create a new behavior.

The idea of a *meaningful experience* allows us to include numerous life changing experiences that people go through, from rites of passage to military training. By adding *the exact following of suggestions* you include the traditional hypnotic experience.

So the key to being good at inducing hypnosis has several components.

1. The hypnotist must get from the hypnotic subject either an overt or implied agreement to follow the suggestions *exactly*.

2. The hypnotist must give acceptable suggestions that will create a *meaningful experience* for the subject.

Before we explore forming acceptable suggestions and how to get agreement to follow them exactly, lets first look at the various other myths of hypnosis.

Mind Control Hypnosis

Who Can and Cannot Be Hypnotized?

People will often ask a hypnotist, "are there people who can't be hypnotized?"

The fact is that the hypnotic state is a *natural* state that people go in and out of all the time. The only real difference is that in hypnosis someone is guiding you through that state.

Consider what happens in those moments before you drift off to sleep. You close your eyes, you still your body, and your attention begins to turn away from the outside world as you fall into an inner world that is all your own. This is very much like the hypnotic state with the exception that *someone is guiding you through that state.*

Understand that everybody can enter that state; therefore, anybody can be hypnotized.

However, whether you, I, or someone else can hypnotize them is a completely different matter. More on this soon.

There are conditions where a person will not respond to hypnosis. These are:

- **People with a low IQ or a brain disorder.**

To be hypnotized you must first have an attention span, and some neurological problems can inhibit one's ability to pay attention. As a general rule these problems must be severe. Schizophrenics already have a tenuous grasp on reality and hypnotizing them is simply best avoided. Attention Deficit Disorder (ADD) is not always enough to prevent hypnosis, although the hypnotist might have to get creative.

Mind Control Hypnosis

- **People drunk or on drugs.**

While alcohol removes inhibitions it does not make hypnosis easier. Most drugs will inhibit the brain from responding to anything. The only exception to this is a rare class of highly controlled drugs called "hypnotics." The most well known is sodium pentathol, also known as "truth serum."

- **Idiots**

I use the term idiots to describe a very small class of people who come to a hypnotist with a complete misconception of hypnosis that even the hypnotist cannot dispel. Even though the hypnotist tells them to "follow the suggestions" and "hypnosis demands your cooperation" they believe that to be convinced they are hypnotized they must be unable to resist the hypnotists suggestions. Thus, they resist all the hypnotists suggestions and they say "I can't be hypnotized."

These latter group of people are thankfully rare and will justify their reactions by what they've seen on TV and in the movies. To them anything that is less than magical, instant, dramatic and puppet-like submission to the hypnotist means they cannot be hypnotized.

- **Children**

Actually, the fact is that most children can be hypnotized. Children have not learned to inhibit their imagination so the truth is that children can't *not* be hypnotized.

Mind Control Hypnosis

Who NOT to Hypnotize

There are many hypnotists in the world who are compassionate, patient, caring and empathetic people and who are usually willing to help anyone with their skills of hypnosis. I am not one of those people.

While I generally like people and love using hypnosis I am also very lazy and don't like to work. There are people who may genuinely want my help but who I've learned to refer to someone else. These people don't fall into a "type," but there are certain behaviors I look out for. Here is my personal list of red flags of people to avoid:

- People who want to negotiate down your fee.

- People consistently late for appointments.

- People who monopolize your time with phone calls and stay beyond the appointment time.

- People who expect you to save them, and those who see themselves as perpetually victimized by the world.

- People who have been diagnosed with borderline personality disorder, as these people will likely demonstrate all of the above behaviors.

The group of people who expect you to save them may seem like good candidates as hypnosis subjects because they would seem to be willing to follow the instructions you give them. While this may be the case on occasion, it is more likely that you will have someone who has a pathological commitment to their own misery.

To explain further, their entire identity is based on a belief that "no one knows my pain," and to remove their pain will leave them in chaos, in spite of what they say. You may help them and for a moment they will notice they are not feeling miserable, but they will then have to create an entirely new perception of who they are. If you help them you may discover that they will begin to instruct you in how everything you are doing to help them is not the right fit for them, but they will still want your help.

If you work with this type of personality it is likely they will begin to cancel out all the good reasons you got into business.

If you have a lot of confidence in your ability you may want to try to help them, but my advise for these people is to quickly and kindly refer them to someone else. It's a good rule to stick with clients whom you can categorize at "the worried well."

Now let's tackle the really *BIG* myth; that people cannot be hypnotized against their will.

Hold on to your seat because most hypnotists won't want you to learn this information.

Mind Control Hypnosis

Can People Be Made To Do Things Against Their Will?

The audience has filled the seats. As the lights go down out steps the gentleman in a tuxedo who invites people to a row of chairs and proceeds to hypnotize them. Because the audience is all over twenty-one the hypnotist goes wild and has his subjects doing the most hilarious and unimaginable things. They seem to be stripped of all inhibitions and common sense. When the show ends people forget the hypnotist's first few words about hypnosis and ask themselves, "can people be made to do things in hypnosis against their will?"

You will not be the first person to ponder that question nor will you be the last.

If you want a short and simple answer to that question the answer is "no," but looking at the question in greater detail can be very interesting and sometimes uncomfortable.

This myth is the reason that people occasionally have an unreasonable fear of hypnosis and hypnotists.

It should be noted that while hypnotists have commonly been feared for willfully controlling their subjects and doing bad things with that control, that fear has not been passed so easily to priests, clergy, doctors and counselors. All of these professions possess an equal power to exploit and abuse their clients, and yet people still fear hypnosis. Strange!

The Myth of The Will

The myth of the Will is that when we focus our intention to make something happen we are exercising our Will.

What one can be capable of by using their Will can inspire awe and wonder. It is by means of Will that nations have been built, buildings raised and fortunes earned...all by shear acts of Will.

The problem with the myth of Will is that, while it can be assumed to exist, very few people use their Will for anything more than getting out of bed and pouring a bowl of cereal.

To really use the Will all one has to do is set an outcome and work to achieve it. The strength of a person's Will, or Will Power, can be measured by how well they accomplish it. Most people will make *some* effort toward their outcome, but sustaining that effort is where most people fall short. They have a Will to stop smoking, to exercise, to lose weight or end an unhealthy habit, but their Will is weak. On the other side of this dynamic think of athletes who want to be Olympic gold medalists. Their Will is set towards one end: being the best they can be in their sport. Every waking moment is spent training and focusing on that goal.

Another example of real Will can be found amid those business people who see a business empire in their future but seem to have few immediate resources. With their Will set, they go about doing whatever needs to be done to work toward the future that they foresee. They plan diligently, learn new skills, create alliances, conserve what they have earned and make necessary sacrifices. If there is a challenge or obstacle they adapt but always with their goal in mind.

So now I ask you, how many people have this later type of Will?

Mind Control Hypnosis

The answer is very, very few.

Most people crumble at their first or second effort. A person wanting to quit smoking lives a week without the habit but upon smoking one cigarette at a bar with friends they deem themselves a failure and give up. They could have taken the event as a lesson and simply recommitted themselves to now lasting even longer, but they do not. They make no effort to see their Will as a muscle to be exercised and strengthened and thus they give up.

Returning now to the question, "can hypnosis make people do things against their will?" the answer is still no, but few people have a Will that is strong enough. If they had enough strength of Will there would be no reason to see a hypnotist.

For a person to prevent herself from being manipulated using hypnosis, or any other modalities of influence, she must have a clear understanding of what she is willing and unwilling to do. In spite of beliefs to the contrary, very few people have that clarity of Will.

Please note that in that previous paragraph the phrase "other modalities of influence" was used. These modalities include religion, psychiatry and social pressure to name a few. While people may shy away from hypnosis as a tool of change they are more than willing to put themselves into situations where there are well documented records of abuse and exploitation. In these other modalities many people have been influenced to do things that they would never have believed they would willingly do. If one is to ask "can hypnosis be used to abuse and injure" they must also be willing to ask if that is true of counseling, psychology and religion.

Mind Control Hypnosis

The problem with entering into any of these modalities on guard and fearful is to limit their effectiveness. There is a certain degree of trust and surrender that is needed to benefit from any modality of influence.

The best advice to give to a person entering into hypnosis is to be very clear on your outcome and be completely willing to follow the suggestions exactly. Trust yourself and the hypnosis process. After all, the best way to judge your success is not during the hypnosis process but upon its completion.

Transference and Values Elicitation

Transference and Values Elicitation are two things that any student of hypnosis should be aware of that can be used to overcome what we think of as the Will. Hypnosis does not have to be taking place to use them. In fact they are used in every other modality of influence (religion, psychiatry, therapy, etc.) often for good and sometimes for bad.

Transference describes what happens in the mind of a client or subject when they begin to project feelings of love and affection onto their therapist. This will often manifest with the client/patient expressing their affection for their counselor/therapist/hypnotist. They may see their therapist as an ideal father figure or mate. The truth is that the therapist is just a person, and while they have as many flaws as anyone else, these flaws are simply unseen. Fortunately, most therapist are well aware of transference and are trained in how to deal with it. They are also aware that it will often happen without the client overtly communicating it.

Using the transference the therapist can do

good things for their clients. They can encourage the client to make changes they would not ordinarily do. They may quit smoking simply because the therapist asked them to regardless of the discomfort quitting smoking may cause.

With this power it's easy to see how even simple transference can be abused.

Therapists, being human, are subject to a similar projection called counter-transference. Counter-transference occurs when the therapist begins to have feelings of affection toward their client. They may look upon their client as a child figure that needs their nurturing or they may see the client as an ideal lover. This, of course, is not real and good therapists are trained to see these "rescue fantasies" for what they are, fanciful creations of the mind.

If you work with a hypnosis client/subject over several sessions you may begin to see this transference manifest. I trust you will use it with the client's well-being in mind.

Values Elicitation

The topic of values elicitation has been thoroughly explained in the book *Mind Control Language Patterns* and reads as follows:

How To Motivate People To Do ANYTHING You Want
Values Elicitation

When you find out what is most important to people, you can use it to influence and persuade them. The power of being able to do this is profound and can be used to help or harm.

The key is to uncover their set of values.

The good news is that it's much easier than you might think. Consider that people love to talk about what is important to them, when someone shows even a little interest. Sometimes, all you have to do is pay attention, and people will give you their hearts (more on this later). Other times, you only need to skillfully ask a few simple questions, and they will tell you everything you want to know about what motivates them.

Here is the process. First, understand that there is a context in which you want to influence the other person. This context could be selling a car, thus the context would be "cars." The context could be seduction, thus you would be talking about "romantic encounters." The rule is to keep the conversation within the context.

Once you are aware of the context, then the question you ask is quite simple. *"What's important to you about (context)?"*

So if the context is cars, then the question would be, "What's important to you about a car?" and if the context is sex, then the question would be, "What's important to you in a lover?"

A variation of this question can be, "When you have (context) fully and completely, what does that give you that's important?"

So, using the examples and this variation, the questions would be, "When you have the car you want, what does that give you that is important?" or, "When you have the lover or sex partner that you truly want, what does that give you that is important?"

When asking these questions, the first answer is not likely to be their deepest value, but it is important. In order to get to their deepest value for this context, you repeat the questioning cycle.

Let's say that your context is seduction, and you are attempting to woo a particular person. The first question asked is, "What's important to you in a lover?" Let us say they answer "romance." So to repeat this process, you would use the word "romance" as they have used it. "When you have romance fully and completely, what does that give you that's important?"

Let's then suppose the person's answer then becomes "passion."

This process of questioning would continue, until you reach their highest value. As a general rule, you will likely only have to repeat this process three times, sometimes less and sometimes more. How will you know their highest value has been reached? Pay attention, and look for some expression of emotion.

Keep in mind that these are people's highest values within this context, and for them to talk about it is bound to elicit emotions of some sort. This emotional response may be subtle or overt. It might not be tears, but you will want to pay attention to their response.

So, knowing that her first answer is "romance" and then "passion," you ask again. "What is ultimately important to you about passion?" Let's suppose their answer is "That would fulfill my deepest desire."

Mind Control Hypnosis

Keep in mind that we are only half way through the entire values elicitation process. Often this first half of the process of elicitation is enough for the person to begin to link these powerful values to you or your product.

Let's continue with the entire process.

Next, you use their answers to link their values to you or your product.

So you know that "romance" and "passion" are part of what makes their vision of an ideal partner and that ,ultimately, passion would "fulfill (her) deepest desire." All you do is work those exact words into the description of your values, or demonstrate them in your behavior.

You might later say something like, "When I think about the things that make a relationship worthwhile, there has to be a feeling of romance and passion, in order to fulfill my deepest desires," or "I don't know how well you can sit there and look at me as we talk, and know that there is, deep inside, a sense of romance and passion that will be there to fulfill your deepest desire."

At first, this may sound mechanical and contrived, but keep in mind that you are talking about their highest values, and it has a very powerful effect.

This pattern is so powerful that it can influence people to do things they would not normally do.

Warning!!!

If this pattern is done to someone in a "dark" way, and they are persuaded to expect something you cannot live up to, then it is likely you will have made an enemy for life - or worse. You may have created someone who is compelled to hunt you down and kill you. Remember, this is manipulation on the level of a person's deepest values.

In short, the process of values elicitation uncovers the subject's deepest values and increases rapport. The result is that the therapist, counselor, priest or salesperson links that value to a suggested outcome. The result is that the subject would believe that by following the suggested behavior they would fulfill that core value. This could be true even if that behavior went against what the subject would usually consider normal or appropriate...and *they don't have to be in hypnosis.*

This later technique of values elicitation has been used by the most skilled negotiators and interrogators in the world with dramatic results. By using values elicitation a person could be made to willingly confess to a crime they did not do. Values elicitation can be use to compel them to commit a crime as long as they believe it would bring them closer to or fulfill a core value.

So, let's ask again, "is it possible to make someone do something against their Will?"

It is possible to have people do things beyond what they think is their normal behavior given several conditions:

- Transference may occur that could compel the subject to do things based on emotions they hold toward their counselor, therapist, priest or hypnotist. They would do it just because the person asked them to do it.

- The subject's core values can be linked to a certain act or behavior so that they feel that by doing this behavior they are fulfilling that value, even while that act might be outside their normal range of behaviors.

- Deception. Never underestimate how much one can be manipulated through deception. Even the famed hypnotherapist, Milton Erickson, was quoted saying "I will go to no end of sophistry to get my client their outcome."

- Very few people truly have the Will needed to train themselves against a skilled combination of Transference, Values Elicitation and deception.

To those who read this for the first time this can be quite a shock, and I know of no other book on hypnosis that has explained it in this way. The author of this book can only encourage you to do nice, healthy and good things with this knowledge, and takes no responsibility for those who, by choice, misuse it.

For the remainder of the book you'll be lead through the process of how the traditional practice of hypnosis can be used to influence people to change, sometimes in dramatic ways. I can only encourage you to use it with wisdom and kindness.

Mind Control Hypnosis

Undressing in Public: An Example of Extreme Hypnosis

There is a 30 minute TV show that stars a famous magician who also claims to be a skilled hypnotist.

In one show he went to a hotel swimming pool and announce he was going to do an hypnosis experiment. By the end of the experiment he had everyone who participated completely naked in a public setting. He proclaimed that no other hypnotist had done that and, to my knowledge, he was right.

The viewer may question whether the event truly occurred as it was portrayed. After all the man is a well known magician, someone who we pay to deceive us. However, based on my experience there were elements of this event that allowed me to believe that what he did was possible. These elements are as follows:

1. Having announced that he was going to do a hypnosis experiment, and offering no other details, he asked for anyone to leave who feels uncomfortable following any outrageous suggestions he might give.
2. After those people left he asked everyone to close their eyes and keep them closed no matter what. Their eyes remained closed throughout the entire experiment.
3. He suggested they bring up feelings of comfort and security, and continued to reinforce these feelings throughout the session.
4. He then told everyone present to remove any clothing they were wearing on the upper torso,

then lower torso. At this point they were completely naked around the hotel pool.
5. He then told them to keep their eyes closed and then redress putting on their bottoms then their tops. Only then did he ask them to open their eyes.

Only when you imagine what the subject's experienced does this begin to seem plausible. First, the hypnosis was to be on *EVERYONE* present. This creates a feeling of group security. No one was present who did not want to participate.

The fact that their eyes were closed during the entire process is important on several levels. First, no one was allowed to be distracted by others looking at them, nor were they distracted by seeing other naked bodies.

Suggesting comfort and security would have added to their ease of undressing.

After the event the participants were amazed that they would have so easily and willingly done such a thing, yet they remember doing it and feeling good about it.

It is these factors that allow me to think that a situation *could* be created where people might be willing to undress in public.

I want to return to what I was saying about using hypnosis with wisdom and kindness. While the thought of this taking place is shocking, the hypnotist used wisdom and kindness in the execution of this naked-at-the-pool hypnosis process. No one was hurt, or embarrassed. Everyone felt a feeling of comfort and security.

As a hypnotist I can say it was beautifully executed.

Mind Control Hypnosis

Overview of The Hypnosis Process

Let me share with you an ironic paradox.

When it comes to hypnosis *people want magic*. To make the most effective hypnosis session there are two thing you must accomplish:

a) Tell them why hypnosis is NOT magical and that the hypnosis process (not you, the hypnotist) demands their full cooperation

and

b) provide them with an experience that seems magical.

When you are able to do this well you'll be very effective at getting the subject to change, and they will be more eager to follow your suggestions.

The following is a detailed description of the procedures that help create that experience for the subject.

The traditional use of hypnosis in the clinical or therapeutic setting consists of several different parts that usually proceed in a sequence. The sequence usually consists of pre-talk, induction and entrainment. The hypnosis process is more detailed, but these three parts are sufficient to help see how it works.

These three aspects of the process each contain opportunities to momentarily bypass the subject's Will and assist in making change happen.

Mind Control Hypnosis

The Pre-talk

The pre-talk is the part of the hypnosis session that precedes the hypnosis. Its purpose is to give the subject enough information to feel comfortable about what will follow and to get the subject's agreement, either explicitly or inferred, to cooperate with the hypnotist and follow the suggestion. The pre-talk itself takes anywhere from two to thirty minutes.

Entrainment

The entrainment teaches the subject how to respond to suggestions by giving them the experience of what it's like.

The Induction

The induction is the process the hypnotist uses to create the hypnotic state. To many it may appear mysterious or hokey, but it is an essential process the subject must go through to achieve hypnosis.

Suggestions

Suggestions is the part where the subject, in hypnosis, is guided through the experience that is designed to be meaningful enough to change their behavior.

The following sections goes into detail using the Dantalion Jones preferred method of hypnosis.

Mind Control Hypnosis

The Pre-Talk

If you've read and listened to as many hypnotists as I have you begin to notice that much of their pre-talk is exactly the same.

Typical pre-talk includes a description of the conscious and unconscious mind. Their abilities and limitations, as well as how they have developed. Also included is how hypnosis relates to the conscious and unconscious minds. The subject is then explained the various responses he or she might have to a suggestion, and which response is optimal for success.

This process can take up to 20 minutes or more depending upon how thorough the hypnotist wants to be with his description.

Upon completion the subject is then asked if they have any questions and if they now are willing to proceed to the hypnosis.

The pre-talk you will get in this book has been tested to be very effective and can help accomplish the desired results in less than two minutes.

Before the pre-talk it's important to talk with the subject to find out what they wish to accomplish. Once the hypnotist is satisfied and feels he has enough information to proceed the pre-talk begins as follows:

"Let me tell you how to be very good at hypnosis. Are you ready?" The hypnotist pauses to get agreement and build anticipation. I recommend you raise your eyebrows and nod your head when asking *"Are you ready?"*

The subject will affirm they are ready.

Take in a deep breath as if you are going to

begin a long monologue and then say *"Follow...my...suggestions."* Say it in a downward tonality. This may bring a laugh to the subject as tension is relieved and here you can turn the tone to more lighthearted. *"Let me explain what that means. If I suggest a thought then think that thought. If I suggest a feeling or emotion then bring forth that feeling. And if I suggest a belief then in that instant imagine that it's absolutely true (pause.) Now let me tell you why this works."*

"As human beings we generally know what we need to do to get what we want but if that information were enough to change us then we would all be rich and thin. So the fact is that information doesn't change our behaviors, What changes our behaviors is having a meaningful experience and that is what we are trying to create in this process. That is why you have to ... follow ... the ... suggestions. I can't give you that experience. I can only guide you. Okay? So as I give a suggestion simply follow it. Don't analyze or judge what you hear just make it true. Agreed?"

There are several reasons that this pre-talk works so let's dissect it in detail.

A primary point is it's brevity. Instead of giving a lot of highly technical and psychological information it is short and understandable.

"Let me tell you how to be very good at hypnosis."

The hypnosis subject is there for a reason, and one you've already uncovered, so it is hoped that their reasons and motivations are transparent. They want a result that will get them what they want. By saying, *"let me tell you how to be very good at hypnosis"* you are presupposing that they can be hypnotized and they can actively take a part in being *"very good'* at it. This gives the subject a feeling of control which they haven't experienced up until this point.

"Are you ready?"

This implies that they have to "get ready" for the information you will give them. The information thus must be important and that their full attention is needed.

"Follow...my...suggestions."

You will find that people will smile or even laugh at times when you say this. The simplicity of the statement *"Follow ... my ... suggestions."* compared to the anticipation they were just feeling creates an emotional "slingshot" much like the punchline of a joke. You are acclimating the subject to be responsive to you with this very simple question and response.

"Let me explain what that means."

This brings the subject back to a slightly more serious matter.

"If I suggest a thought then think that thought. If I suggest a feeling or emotion then bring forth that feeling. And if I suggest a belief then in that instant imagine that it's absolutely true."

Mind Control Hypnosis

Very simple and explicit instructions yet not condescending. It explains everything the subject must do in the areas of thought, emotions and belief.

You will at times get a subject who doesn't understand how they would "make a belief true" if they didn't believe it to begin with. I deal with this by asking them "just suppose for a moment you absolutely *knew* that something wonderful was about to happen. What would it be like?" They would then describe what would be different with them if that were true. I would then go on to explain "to know what it would be like if you know something wonderful was about to happen you had to, at some level, put yourself in that state. That's all I'm asking you to do is "just suppose" a belief is true the moment I suggest it."

"Now let me tell you why this works.

"As human beings we generally know what we need to do to get what we want, but if that information were enough to change us then we would all be rich and thin. So the fact is that information doesn't change our behaviors. What changes our behavior is having a meaningful experience, and that is what we are trying to create in this process. That is why you have to...follow...the...suggestions. I can't give you that experience. I can only guide you. Okay? So as I give a suggestion simply follow it. Don't analyze or judge what you hear. Just make it true. Agreed?"

The beauty of this last paragraph is it's logical simplicity. It speaks to everyone's experience and addresses in short order the complaint "I know *what* to do. I just can't seem to do it." The reason is that "knowledge" has a very limited effect on behavior. It also reemphasizes that the subject must take control by following the suggestions the hypnotist gives them.

This pre-talk explains and upholds the definition of hypnosis that has been given, "*hypnosis is the exact following of suggestions to create a meaningful experience.*"

The next step of the hypnosis process, called "The Entrainment" is something I've only seen a few hypnotists do but adds to the effectiveness of the hypnosis by a hundred fold.

Mind Control Hypnosis

The Entrainment

The purpose of the Entrainment is to teach the subject how to respond to suggestions. Through the pre-talk the subject has an understanding of what it means to "follow the suggestions," but they do not have an experience of it.

The Entrainment would immediately follow the pre-talk.

"Okay, let me show you how to respond when you hear a suggestion. I'm going to give you some suggestions right now and when you hear them, don't judge, don't analyze or evaluate them. Don't even think. Just do them the instant you hear them. Okay, let's go. Lift your arm. Look up. Look down. Close your eyes. Nod your head. Say 'elephant'."

The delivery of these commands should be done in quick succession but with a flat tonality as if ordering from a menu. They are best done without gesture or pantomime. Having done it the first time have them do it again. This will give them a second chance to do it better.

"Let's do that again, even better. Lift your arm. Look up. Look down. Close your eyes. Nod your head. Say 'elephant'."

Keeping in mind our definition of hypnosis. *"Hypnosis is the exact following of suggestions to create a meaningful experience."* One can see how the entrainment adheres to *"the exact following of suggestions"* and helps makes it possible.

What follows the Entrainment is the hypnotic

induction.

Ultimately the goal of entrainment is to have a subject that is unconditionally responsive to your suggestions. This ideal can only be achieved through practice and repetition.

There is an interesting subset of individuals who don't respond to hypnosis because they regard hypnosis with strong unaltered misconceptions. They believe that they could only be under hypnosis if they are unable to resist the hypnotists suggestions, therefore they make every effort to **not** do what the hypnotist suggests. This is not following the hypnotists suggestion but challenging them. Fortunately, these people are rare and their misconceptions can usually be removed with a little more education and through the process of entrainment.

Using Reward and Punishment

There are hypnotists who use both reward and punishment to reach a high level of entrainment. The reward is, at the very least, an acknowledging word or a suggestion to feel a pleasant feeling. The punishment can vary widely from a stern word to a complete torture session. It should be noted that using punishment more severe than simple silence, as a tool for hypnotic compliance is at best a morally questionable practice.

Those who use punishment to create compliance are not professional hypnotists or coaches but consider themselves to be "trainers" and "programmers". They often are employed by clandestine organizations that are usually involved in criminal endeavors. Those "trainers" will also end

Mind Control Hypnosis

a traumatic session with comfort items.

Comfort items are offered to the subject when their training session is completed. By doing this the subject begins to identify with the programmer in a condition called the Stockholm syndrome, and confuses the subject as to the motivations of the trainer. The process assists the subject to put aside any feelings of the trauma. In short, it is an extreme way to mess up someone's mind.

Consider how a fraternity or organization may put an initiate through a difficult initiation but up completing the initiation they are "bonded" to the group with celebration and mass approval and support. This celebration is a variation of the "comfort item".

Mind Control Hypnosis

The Hypnotic Induction

The hypnotic induction has been describe as a ritual for the benefit of the subject and, like many other rituals, is designed to introduce a change in experience.

The induction that follows is a modified version of the traditional Elman induction.

"Closer your eyes, pay attention to all the muscles of the forehead, and let those muscles completely relax... and recognize that to be successful at any hypnosis process is very simple, all you have to do is follow the suggestions. So, if a thought is suggested then think the thought. If a feeling or emotion is suggested then bring forth the feeling and, if a belief is suggested then in that moment imagine it to be absolutely true."

"So create for yourself a feeling of ease and comfort, a feeling that is even more enjoyable than just a moment ago. When you notice that feeling take in a deep breath and as you let it out and settle into that feeling of ease and comfort. (pause until subject exhales with a sigh)...and recognize that you created that feeling. You are the one in complete control. You created the feeling. You simply followed the suggestion."

"And notice as you are relaxing even deeper how easily the eyes and eyelids just naturally...stay closed...relax the eyes and eyelids even further so that they just continue to...remain closed...Let you eyes gently roll up and gaze toward the middle of the forehead and in a voice within your mind tell the eyelids to...remain closed...no...matter...what...and seal the eyes so tightly shut no one can open them...

so tightly sealed even you cannot open them...make that true and it becomes true...and when you have take a instant and prove it to yourself...and then stop...take a deep breath...and...relax even deeper. The eyelids stay closed because you make it so...you are the one in complete control...you simply followed the suggestions."

"Now as relaxed as you are double it...(pause) then...double it again...and begin now to imagine yourself playing a child's game...where you find yourself...inside your mind...standing with your eyes closed...and you begin to spin in a circle...laughing and giggling as you spin and spin and spin and all of the world simply falls away. Keep spinning and spinning...again and again...around and around and around and around...and then you...stop...and there in front of you is a black box...an ordinary black box no more than knee high...until you open it and it's filled with a vast emptiness in which you can throw anything and it will simply...fall away...so you throw away all your worries, doubts and hesitations...and if you like...throw away all your conscious awareness and seal up the box...seal it tighter than you've sealed your eyes shut...and then again you close your eyes and begin again to turn and spin around and around, spinning and spinning and all of the conscious awareness falls away..."

With the induction presented we can now analyze its parts.

"Closer your eyes pay attention to all the muscles of the forehead and let those muscles completely relax...and recognize that to be successful at any hypnosis process is very simple.

Mind Control Hypnosis

All you have to do is follow the suggestions. So, if thought is suggested then think the thought. If a feeling or emotion is suggested then bring forth the feeling and, if a belief is suggested then in that moment imagine it to be absolutely true."

In this first paragraph the instructions to "follow the suggestions" is reiterated as in the pre-talk and explained exactly what is needed to do so.

"So create for yourself a feeling of ease and comfort a feeling that is even more enjoyable than just a moment ago. When you notice that feeling take in a deep breath and as you let it out and settle into that feeling of ease and comfort. (pause until subject exhales with a sigh)...and recognize that you created that feeling. You are the one in complete control. You created the feeling. You simply followed the suggestion."

This step does two things. First, it allows the hypnotist to know that the subject if following the suggestion by noticing the deep breath. Secondly. It demonstrates to the subject that they are in control of their success.

"And notice as you are relaxing even deeper how easily the eyes and eyelids just naturally...stay closed... relax the eyes and eyelids even further so that they just continue to...remain closed...Let you eyes gently roll up and gaze toward the middle of the forehead and in a voice within your mind tell the eyelids to...remain closed...no...matter...what...and seal the eyes so tightly shut no one can open them...so tightly sealed even you cannot open...make

that true and it becomes true...and when you have take a instant and prove it to yourself...and then stop...take a deep breath...and...relax even deeper. The eyelids stay closed because you make it so...you are the one in complete control...you simply followed the suggestions."

This is the part of the induction that is the modified Elman hypnotic induction. As you have demonstrated with the previous paragraph, the subject is in complete control, thus they must have the control to create this sensory paradox. By extension, if they can create this sensory paradox, then they follow other suggestions with ease. It further reiterates that, by following the suggestions, they are the ones in control of the experience.

"Now as relaxed as you are, double it...(pause) then...double it again...and begin now to imagine yourself playing a child's game...where you find yourself...inside your mind...standing with your eyes closed...and you begin to spin in a circle...laughing and giggling as you spin and spin and spin and all of the world simply falls away. Keep spinning and spinning...again and again...around and around and around and around...and then you...stop..."

This part of the hypnosis session is referred to as the "deepener." The deepener is typically the part where the hypnotist counts down from ten to one telling the subject to "deepen" the relaxation/hypnosis/trance.

What I've found by doing this form of deepener is that it relies on the disorienting experience of spinning to pull the subject out an ordinary state of awareness. Combined with the fact that they are asked to close their imaginary eyes and do it all within their imagination, their mind is fully occupied within this internal state.

"...and there in front of you is black box...an ordinary black box no more than knee high...until you open it and it's filled with a vast emptiness in which you can throw anything and it will simply...fall away...so you throw away all your worries, doubts and hesitations...and if you like...throw away all your conscious awareness and seal up the box...seal it tighter than you've sealed your eyes shut...and then again you close your eyes and begin again to turn and spin around and around, spinning and spinning and all of the conscious awareness falls away..."

The black box metaphor is used to further distance the subject from their worries and concerns as well as assist the hypnotist by getting rid of the subject's doubts and hesitations. The subject is encouraged, but not commanded, to put their conscious awareness within the box as well. This can help the subject by getting rid of any possible conscious objection to the suggestions that will be given.

Once again, the subject performs the spinning process.

Before going into the portion of the hypnosis where the therapeutic suggestions are given the next section will discuss the "tricky" aspects of hypnosis that help compel the subject to follow all the hypnotists suggestions...no matter what!

This, of course, is just one variation of

hypnosis induction. Another method involves an induction and awakening process that have identical elements. In the following example the "black pearl" is used. Having common elements at the beginning and ending of the hypnosis can create a kind of "container" in which the other suggestion are held.

Upon awakening the subject will tend to only remember the common elements that are shared in the induction and awakening.

The Black Pearl Induction with Awakening

(Ellipses, or three dots in this script do not indicate missing parts, but rather pauses. In other words, pauses are indicated by three dots.)

"Breathe deeply. You are floating down...down...on a beautiful red cloud, and your whole body is red...as you go drifting and floating...rocking gently...deeper...and deeper...down..."(this repeated, one time, for each color of cloud-orange, yellow, green, blue, and violet clouds.)

"Land very gently...very softly...in the center of a round, black pearl. See it glowing, softly, gently. Now turn and face the East...and then the South...and then the West...and then the North. Open all of your inner senses." (The rainbow gives the subject a safe mental place to travel to; and this serves as a "home base" for the mind to return to if things get difficult.)

Bringing The Subject Out Of Trance

After the suggestions have been made it is important

that the programmer takes time to get the subject to emerge slowly and gently from their altered state. The induction process is reversed. The repetition of trances will reinforce the depth of the trance state, and keep everything operating smoothly:

"In the pearl prepare to awaken. When you awake, you will feel refreshed, alert, renewed, and filled with energy. You will remember all that you have experienced. Now turn and face the East...then the South...then the West...then the North." (This helps the subject orient themselves internally.)

"Take a deep breath...inhale...exhale. You are floating up...up...on a beautiful violet cloud, and your whole body is violet as you drift gently upward on a beautiful blue cloud...up...up...and your whole body is blue and you are beginning to awaken gently and you drift gently up...up...on a beautiful green cloud...and your whole body is green...as you drift gently...up...up...on a beautiful yellow cloud...getting more and more awake...and your whole body is yellow...as you drift gently...up...up...on a beautiful orange cloud...filled with energy and vitality...your whole body is orange...as you float up gently...on a beautiful red cloud...almost fully awake now...and your whole body is red as you float gently. Stay on the rainbow."

After the session the hypnotist finishes...

"Leaving the memory in the black pearl and closing and sealing the black pearl you will remember only those details that I tell you to remember, and in a moment you will count to ten and go back into your space, and return."

Mind Control Hypnosis

Five Things That Assist To Induce Hypnosis

The nature of the mind is such that it will respond to certain events and actions by creating a state that is very susceptible to suggestion. These events and actions are *relaxation, surprise, physical disorientation, confusion and emotions.* When you understand how these situations effect the mind you'll be better able to induce hypnosis in others.

Relaxation

The neophyte to hypnosis is most often introduced to hypnotic induction by means of relaxation. This is where the subject is guided through a relaxation process starting at one end of the body and slowly progressing through the parts of the body to the other end.

The reason this works is that by relaxing the body it is supposed to remove resistance to any suggestions.

The downside of a hypnotic induction that uses relaxation is that it sometimes puts the subject into a state of sleep instead of hypnosis. Many hypnotists become "married" to the progressive relaxation induction and unknowingly limit themselves because it does not easily lend itself to testing the hypnotic state.

Surprise

When a person experiences surprise they are forced to make sense of the experience. This pushes out all other distractions and forces their awareness to a single focus.

Mind Control Hypnosis

The most common hypnotic induction process using surprise is when the hypnotist shouts "SLEEP!" at the subject. With few exceptions this will seldom work without the pre-talk.

Physical Disorientation

Most people have experienced the sensations of swinging on a swing and closing their eyes. Likewise you may have sat in a rotating chair and spun around with your eyes closed. The experience tends turn ones attention inward and away from the external environment. This is an ideal inroads to create a meaningful internal experience for the hypnotist.

Some cultures would do this by building a "witches chair." This is a comfortable chair or bed that is suspended from the ceiling. The subject would close their eyes and others would swing and rotate the chair as the subject focused on creating an meaningful internal mental state.

In modern hypnosis there are inductions which rely on very gently rocking the subject as you give suggestions. The rocking or movement is not so much for the standing subject to fall over (the hypnotists arm is holding them steady by the shoulders) but it is just enough to create a gentle disorientation.

Confusion

If you have ever experienced something confusing it is not pleasant. In the state of confusion the mind will quickly begin to search for anything that will help make sense of the situation. This search seldom takes more than a second but within the brief moment the mind is highly suggestible and will accept any suggestion that might fit.

It should be noted that surprise, physical disorientation and confusion make up many of the rapid hypnotic inductions. These will be discussed in the next section.

Emotions

Hypnotic Inductions that use emotions are seldom used by anyone other than the most skilled hypnotists and are often used to deal with severe emotional pain and trauma.

To understand how emotions are used to induce hypnosis one can start by understanding that emotional reactions are seldom within our conscious control and have their origins deep within the unconscious mind. When someone is beginning to feel and express an emotion they have pushed aside most other distractions and are becoming very focused.

A skilled hypnotist will use this focus as a starting point for the induction by asking the subject to focus on the feeling and it's origins. Most often this emotion will be based in pain or fear. The hypnotist's intent would be to remove the negative emotion and help the subject reframe the experience.

The use of an emotion based hypnotic induction is best left to the skilled and experienced professionals who know how to deal with pain and trauma.

Mind Control Hypnosis

A Comment on Inductions

People are not cookies cut from the same mold so you will find that some people respond better to one induction process than another. You may find some subjects get nauseous when they imagine themselves spinning, for example, so be flexible.

You will find that your best work comes from your most challenging subjects. Take it in stride and adapt.

You may also find that some subjects respond better to a long drawn out induction that includes lots of counting backwards.

Once you've worked with a subject enough times it's likely they will have learned how to enter the hypnotic state at will and very rapidly. Even when they have reached that level of skill as a hypnosis subject you are still likely to hear from them the best ways to phrase their suggestions.

In the next section we'll discuss inducing hypnosis in the most rapid ways imaginable.

Mind Control Hypnosis

Rapid Hypnotic Inductions

A rapid induction is very dramatic to watch and many stage hypnotists have use this type of induction to bill themselves as "the worlds fastest hypnotist".

A rapid hypnotic induction typically takes anywhere from 5 to 30 seconds to perform and can seem very foreboding to the neophyte because it demands a great deal of confidence and boldness to perform.

To understand how to use rapid inductions let's talk about *why* it works.

First understand that the human nervous system has it's own limitations. When a person is shocked or threatened all awareness stops. The attention then quickly turns into a search to understand what is happening and to choosing the right response. A rapid induction exploits this weakness by creating an unexpected shock where attention halts momentarily, and then quickly providing the response by offering a suggestion,

A description of the rapid induction will soon follow but it can seem so bold that even the most detailed description may seem inadequate, especially to those who have not done it. Others who resist using the rapid induction will do so simply because it is so dramatic and resembles a stage show. I've heard people object to rapid inductions because it would make them appear as if they are showing off.

Personally, I'm more concerned about what is effective, and what other people think be damned.

Mind Control Hypnosis

Components of the Rapid Induction

As simple as the rapid induction is, it has components that will help to make it work more effectively.

The components are The Set Up, The Shock, and The suggestion/Entrainment

1. The Set Up or Pre-talk

This is your typical pre-talk as mentioned earlier. Ask the subject to agree to follow your suggestions and get their complete agreement. This is often done without telling them the induction method they are going to use.

2. The Shock

Most often the shock is a quick motion or shout. It is most commonly done by the hypnotist extending his hand as to begin a handshake. When the subject follows through with the handshake the hypnotist jerks their clasped hands and shouts in a commanding voice "SLEEP!" Then reaches up to the subjects face to close their eyes and continue with the suggestions.

3. The Suggestion/Entrainment

The suggestion phase is much like any suggestion phase with the suggestions proceeding fluidly.

For those hypnotists doing this type of rapid induction for the first time they often are so shocked

Mind Control Hypnosis

by it's effectiveness and speed they are at a loss for what to say. Knowing this ahead of time you can be ready to continue with your suggestions.

That is the whole of the rapid induction. It is so simple, short and surprising that it is hard to believe, yet it's that effective.

Here is what it would sound like if you were to overhear this rapid induction being used.

"... so do I have your agreement to follow my suggestions?"

(wait for agreement)

"Great!"

(hypnotist extends hand for a handshake, subject grasps hands)

"SLEEP!"

(hypnotist give one swift short jerking pull on the subjects hand.)

"Let your eyes close... tighter and tighter ... so tight perhaps not even you can open them ... but for now just relax and follow my words as if they were your own thoughts..."

Once you have the idea of how rapid inductions work you can also begin to improvise and create your own variation.

Variation #1

Ask the subject to close their eyes while standing and then rock them with your hands on their shoulders.

Variation #2

Tell the subject you will not let them fall. Have them stand and close their eyes while facing you.

Mind Control Hypnosis

Put your hands on their shoulders and ask them to lean in to you. Let them lean more and more and when they are getting comfortable with that position let your arm break so that they fall forward. Command them to "Sleep!" and catch them so they do not hit the ground.

From these examples, and a little bit of experience, you can pretty quickly begin to create your own variations of rapid hypnotic induction.

Mind Control Hypnosis

Subtle "Tricks" Within The Hypnosis Process

The "tricks" that follow in this chapter are done during the hypnosis process to increase the subject's compliance to the hypnotists suggestions. Some of them are simply observations about the normal hypnosis process that are done in most any hypnotic session. Others are processes or hypnotic suggestions to be made.

Overcoming The Will by Agreement

As mentioned earlier, at some level the subject must agree to follow the hypnotists suggestions. This has been often referred to as "the hypnotic agreement."

When you read the pre-talk consider the fact that the hypnotic agreement bypasses the Will because of the subject's motivation (or perhaps through the guile and trickery of the hypnotist), and agrees to *follow the suggestion exactly* in order to have the experience that will benefit them.

By comparison, there is a difference between the hypnotic agreement and what happens in other psychotherapies. In other psychotherapies the subject is generally not asked to blindly follow the therapist. The only agreement the subject has to the traditional therapist is to show up on time and pay their bill. Typically the subject/patient must pour over events and emotions so that if they are to make any change they must discover it themselves. In classic Freudian psychoanalysis the therapist is forbidden from doing anything greater than asking, "and how did you feel about that?"

The result is that the traditional therapist

often has to fight the Will of the subject to get any change to occur.

Overcoming Will by linking pleasure and good things

If you've ever experienced hypnosis you will likely agree it is a very pleasant and enjoyable experience.

There are several reasons for this. The relaxed state is free from tension, the general awareness of the world is absent, and pleasant feelings can be suggested and amplified.

Any pleasant emotion or feeling that can be experienced by the subject can be amplified. Also, any pleasant feeling can be linked to anything else; a thought, an action, a belief.

The "trick" is to purposefully link pleasant feelings to every step of the hypnosis process, and especially to the simple act of following the hypnotist's suggestions. This process begins at the very start of the hypnotic induction where the subject is asked to *"create for yourself a feeling of ease and comfort, a feeling that is even more enjoyable than just a moment ago.'* From there the *"ease and comfort'* can be increased and altered.

An example of this type of suggestion would be as follows:

"As you notice that feeling of joy and pleasure take a moment to settle into it and understand that whenever you say the words, "I'm a nonsmoker." Whether aloud or in your mind you can feel that joy and pleasure increasing more and more with every passing day. So take a moment now and feel that joy

and pleasure and repeat in your mind those pleasing words, "I'm a nonsmoker. I'm a nonsmoker. I'm a nonsmoker." Repeating repeating right now, out loud to yourself inside like a gentle echo. Just let this voice be in the background of your thoughts reminding you of that joy and pleasure as you hear 'I'm a nonsmoker. I'm a nonsmoker. I'm a nonsmoker.' The louder you hear it the more joy you feel."

To the hypnotist who wants to use this consider all the things that you suggest and all the possible pleasant feelings that could be linked to each other.

The Emotional Chamber

Another example of the amplification and linking of emotions was created by JD Fuentes, the author of a book on relationships and seduction titled "The Sexual Key System." Fuentes named this process "The Emotional Chamber," and while it mimics the female sexual response it should be noted that it is a very effective process regardless of the subject's gender. The Emotional Chamber can be used effectively in hypnosis to amplify the quality of emotions.

The steps are as follows:

1. Bring in or become aware of a pleasurable feeling or emotion.
2. Create an opening, like a door, through which the subject can bring in this emotion.
3. Amplify the emotion and describe it in other

sensory modalities, visual, auditory, kinesthetic, etc.
4. Bring that feeling/emotion to a peak.
5. This then invites in another emotion.
6. Repeat the process using this new feeling/emotion.

As part of a hypnosis script it would sound something like this:

"As you hear those words repeating in your mind, "I'm a non-smoker. I'm a non-smoker. I'm a non-smoker." Invite a feeling of satisfaction in as if you were to open a door and bring in that warm, fuzzy feeling of satisfaction. And let that satisfaction begin to grow stronger and stronger growing to a peak and as it culminates you feel that wonderful feeling of relief. So create an opening and let the relief come in and let it build growing stronger and stronger with a satisfying tingle that moves through every part of you... building... beyond belief...(etc.)"

This cycle can be repeated with any number of emotions and creates a very powerful and positive feeling within the subject, and again links it to the needed state or new response.

The Hypnotic Yes Set

In sales there is something called "the yes set," which is a series of questions to which the answer is consistently "yes." In the Hypnotic "Yes Set" multiple pleasant emotions and feelings are elicited and then linked to the subject saying the word "yes." The pleasure of saying yes to the

Mind Control Hypnosis

hypnotist's questions and suggestions can become a pleasantly compulsive response and thus aid in the subjects compliance to the suggestions.

The suggestions may be phrased like this:

In a moment I'm going to ask you to bring up a very positive feeling of ease and comfort and when you feel that wonderful feeling simply say the word "Yes." So begin now to build that wonderful feeling and let it come to a peak and at it's peak let me know by saying "yes"...(Pause until the subject says yes. If too much time seems to pass continue to encourage and lead)...Yes, that's right. As you now feel that sense of ease and comfort bring a feeling of relief...and when you feel that sense of relief make it real and say "yes"(pause)...and now combine that ease and comfort with that sense of relief...bring them together and as you notice that they have merged and increased say the word..."yes." (pause) Now, bring in the feeling of...pleasure...wonderful shear...pleasure and when you've brought in that...pleasure...say yes...and notice how easy and pleasurable it is now to speak to me in wonderful state...do you enjoy this feeling? (wait for a "yes") Can you now increase that pleasure even more now? (wait for "yes) Good! Double that pleasure and bring to this the feeling of rightness...that this is a joy and pleasure and when you notice that feeling of rightness say "yes." Double that feeling again and say "yes." (pause) Do you enjoy this feeling? (pause) Do you enjoy this process (pause)...and following each suggestion...? (pause) that you hear from me...? Now just as you feel that feeling of pleasure...make that feeling present...with each suggestion you follow. Do you agree?"

Mind Control Hypnosis

The hypnotist can make an entire session that creates and amplifies pleasure while linking that pleasure to following the suggestions.

Variation #2 "Open Your Eyes"

This variation of the "Yes Set" should be used with a great deal of caution because it can create a very strong transference toward the hypnotist.

The difference is that instead of asking the subject to say "Yes" when the pleasurable state is achieved the hypnotist asks the subject to open their eyes. The hypnotist will place themselves in direct line of sight to the subject and by default be the first person the subject will see when this ideal pleasurable state is reached. In so doing the pleasurable feeling is linked to the hypnotist. This is all done without the hypnotist overtly telling the subject to "link those powerful feelings to me."

This should be done with great caution and perhaps not at all, for it can create a very compulsive subject who constantly wants the attention of the hypnotist, which can be quite an annoyance if one does not know how to handle a client/subject who feel a strong sense of transference. It can also be very easy for a hypnotist to "forget" the *en loco parentus* responsibility they have.

Before you attempt this for the first time it is wise to repeat several times the words of Spiderman, "with great power comes great responsibility."

Mind Control Hypnosis

Overcoming Will by minute progress

"The journey of a thousand miles begins with a single step."

So it is through taking small, simple, and incremental steps that someone can be lead into a hypnotic state where they could potentially do *any behavior* the hypnotist asks of them.

Think about what you've learned so far and the implications of it being applied perfectly to the right person.

1. They would agree to follow the suggestions and have a basic understanding of what that would be needed.

2. Using the modified Elman induction they would be shown how to create the paradox of sealing their eyes so that even they could not open them. This offers an example that they can seemingly do strange and wonderful things.

3. They are told to bring up a positive emotion and to amplify it, again demonstrating the control that they have. This for many is enough to willingly follow the suggestions.

4. Take that pleasure and link it to an act or behavior, the hypnotists voice, or to simply following suggestions without question.

Each step is a small and incremental one, yet each has it's purpose and lays a foundation for the next step.

Mind Control Hypnosis

This is how people are hypnotically trained, whether for therapeutic reasons or for entertainment. It also describes how most hypnosis sessions proceed.

At this point the implications of this information could frighten many lay people. It could equally anger many hypnotists because it implies that a person *could* be compelled to do things in hypnosis contrary to their normal behavior, but the fact is *that is why hypnosis is such a powerful tool of behavioral change*. If a persons normal behavior is smoking, overeating and lack of self confidence then hypnosis may be the best and fastest tool for the job.

Let's consider someone who enters traditional therapeutic modalities because they lack confidence when they are with people they find attractive. Psychoanalysis can takes months or years to achieve a noticeable result. Other therapies can have varying results. The reason is that most therapies have to battle their way past all the conscious barriers the subject/patient has learned. These barriers may be simple habits or they may be beliefs about their self worth and deservingness.

Hypnosis is about training new reactions and responses so that they happen automatically. While the training may happen in one hypnosis session or several the time by comparison is much less that other therapies.

Mind Control Hypnosis

Tips, Techniques, and Interesting Tricks of The Hypnotist

This chapter contains some of the "insider techniques" that I've developed as a hypnotist and in talking with experimental hypnotists over the years.

These insider techniques are ideas used in hypnosis that aid the subject to be more compliant. They are also metaphors that the hypnotist can use to simplify the giving and accepting of suggestions.

Each one of these has it's benefits and will be explained in detail. You'll probably find that you can incorporate them as language patterns in more conversational formats.

Using The Subject's Own Words

If you have studied the use of values elicitation (see the book **Mind Control Language Patterns**) you find that by using the subject's exact words you can unlock very powerful emotions. This affect is increased when used in hypnosis.

It is assumed that the hypnotist would have taken some time prior to the hypnosis session to talk with the subject. During that time the hypnotist would have heard how they describe their problem and what it does to them. They would have also heard what feelings they would feel to be free of the problem.

As a hypnotist, and a lazy one at that, I make it a point to jot down any of the key words, sometimes called "trance words" that the subject uses to describe their internal states and emotions. It is not uncommon to get a profound response when these words are used in hypnosis. After solving a problem for them a subject may cry with relief at the hearing of these words.

Pointing Out Successes and Using Them

The technical term for this is Trance Ratification and it is a process that provides the subject with a convincer that they are in some different state of awareness. You will find that sometimes even the most skilled hypnotic subject will not believe they were in an altered state. So when you have the subject experience or do something that is outside their normal experience and behavioral they take note. In that experience their confidence is built and the experience can be referred to in the future.

An example of trance ratification is the hypnotic induction where first the subject creates a feeling of ease and comfort and then is told to seal his eyes shut so that he could not open them. When the subject follows these two suggestions the hypnotist points out that the subject, not the hypnotist, created those results. This ability of the subject will be referenced throughout the session.

As an example such a hypnotic script would be:

"Now link that pleasure to these words repeating in your mind, 'I'm a non-smoker. I'm a non-smoker. I'm a non-smoker.' Just like a moment ago you made it true the eyes would stay closed no matter how hard you tried, make it true that these words 'I'm a non-smoker' bring you such joy, relief and pleasure...every time you say those words to yourself."

Mind Control Hypnosis

This gives the subject a ratification of trance and an example of how to treat other suggestions.

The Voice of Experience

The "Voice of Experience" mentioned in the book *Mind Control Language Patterns* is a conversational tool of influence, but its effectiveness can be easily multiplied when used in hypnosis.

Here is the hypnosis version of The Voice of Experience.

"Within the mind reside incredible and wonderful resources that are there for us to use. Some of those wonderful resources are memories. We all have memories of times we've learned, and maybe you can even remember your very earliest memory of learning when you learned what it was like to learn. Maybe you were with a group of people or with someone older, but in that moment you knew what it was like to learn, and everything seemed right. It sounded true and it felt real."

"In a lot of ways it's like this voice - a voice of experience and support. So when you think about what it is you're going to learn and you listen you can hear this voice...and if you listen...really listen...you can hear this voice right now...speaking to you right from the very center of who you are. This is your voice of experience and support. I have a voice like that and you have this voice too...and even in the quiet moments of your thoughts you can always hear this voice...guiding you, protecting you and keeping you from harm."

Mind Control Hypnosis

You'll note that there is nothing in this pattern that directly says, "my voice is the voice in your head," but when someone is hearing this pattern, at some level, they put in the speakers voice as that "voice of experience." In fact anytime the hypnotist refers to an inner voice as "this voice" they are relying on an ambiguity to take place. Does "this voice" mean the voice in my head or the voice of the hypnotist? Not knowing which answer to accept the mind agrees that it means both.

Some of the variations of this can be very direct. I've heard some hypnotist simply say *"make my voice your inner voice,'* and this *will* work for those who prefer brute force over subtlety.

When this is done on a recording that the subject will hear repeatedly the effect can be that they instantly begin to respond to the hypnotists voice in any situation. When listening to bedtime hypnosis sessions, some female subjects will report lightheartedly to their hypnotists that "I go to sleep to you every night."

Mind Control Hypnosis

Places In The Mind

This next processes can be quite useful for both the hypnotist and the subject because it creates a quick and effective way to deal with *anything* that the subject brings to the hypnosis session.

To get a clear image of this concept, here is a quote that you might ponder: *"To name something is to make it real. To describe it makes it come alive."* This becomes even more true in the highly suggestible state of hypnosis.

If this is true then it is possible to create things or places within the mind that can go to work for the subject as needed. All that needs to be done is to fully describe how these things or places in the mind work.

While there are many possibilities, what follows are four specific "places in the mind" that can be created in hypnosis and used to great effect. With each you'll get the description that "make it come alive." With each of these places within the mind it is recommended that upon creating them you also test them out as well.

They are:

1. The place where things are true.
2. The place where things only used to be true but aren't any longer.
3. The place where anything is possible and can be made true.
4. The place of forgetting.

One way to introduce this concept to the subject is by simply saying, *"we all have places in the mind. One of those places in the mind is..."*

Mind Control Hypnosis

The Place Where Things Are True

"The Place Where Things Are True" is where the hypnotist wants all of his/her suggestions to go. The description of "The Place Where Things are True" would sound something like this:

"We all have places in the mind. One of those places in the mind is the place where things are true. This is where we put thing we know are absolutely true, like the sun rises in the east and sets in the west or that the earth id below and the sky above. Find this place where things are true. Think of one thing you know is true...perhaps it's that you have feelings for someone dear to you...or that breathing clear air is good...and when you have this place where things are true simply nod your head...(wait)...In this place where things are true you can put anything there and it becomes true."

This is enough to create The Place Where Things Are True, and to let it come alive. From here all the suggestions can be placed there.

"...take that belief that says 'I am a non-smoker' and place it in that place where things are true...and notice how...it just fits...and when you've noticed that just nod your head."

Even the hypnotists voice can come from the Place Where Things Are True.

"...and as you listen, listen, listen to every word repeating in your mind notice how this voice

comes right from that place where things are true... and it's there guiding you, encouraging you, comforting you and keeping you from harm..."

The Test for The Place Where Things Are True

"...now take those words 'I'm a non-smoker' and place it in that place where you everything you know is true and make it fit perfectly...notice how it feels there...where things are true...and when you have it there so that it feels just right...simply nod your head..."

With those final instructions to nod their head when "it feels just right" is the sign that they have done it correctly, and that their "test" is complete.

The Place Where Things Used To Be True

Throughout our lives things change. We go to school, and learn to drive. Move from one town to another, one apartment to another, and during these changes what once used to be true for us isn't true any longer.

We used to go to high school but now we don't.

We used to drive a red mustang but now we don't.

We used to live in a specific apartment but now we don't.

All of these things fit into a special place in our mind where things *use to be true* but aren't any longer.

So it is that once we recognize this place where things used to be true we can begin to put thing there that we no longer want to be true. We can put beliefs and habits there.

For example, if you put the belief that "dieting is painful" there it would make losing weight much more enjoyable. The same would be true if you put the love of chocolate there. From that point in time onward the subject would know that they *used to believe* that dieting was painful, but not any longer. They would remember that they *used to* love chocolate but now it's no big deal.

To create this place in the mind the hypnosis script would be something like follows.

"...there is also a place where you put things that only used to be true but aren't any longer. Like you used to ride a certain bicycle but now you don't or you used to live in an apartment but not any more...in this place are all the things that used to be true but aren't any longer...take a moment to find this place where things used to be true...and when you do nod your head..."

The Test For The Place Where Things Used To Be True

"Now take that habit of smoking and the belief that quitting smoking is hard and place it in that place where you put things that used to be true... notice how it feels ... you used to smoke... you used to believe that quitting smoking is hard ... but not any more .... and make all the adjustments so that it fits and it feels just right there... and when you have simply nod your head."

You can further test it through questioning. *"You notice how good it feels there? Yes?"*

Mind Control Hypnosis

The Place Where *Anything* Is Possible

This place, where *anything* is possible is quite powerful because it is there that dramatic changes can be made and tested out before bringing them into the everyday world.

As an example of the place where anything is possible in action you might consider how people (perhaps even yourself) have changed to enjoy things that at one time would have never been considered. The most dramatic of these can be how some people at one time in their lives could never consider certain sexual acts but after being in a relationship that act becomes a pleasant norm.

Somewhere within their mind they began to consider it as a possibility and, in that place, they played with it until they were willing to accept it.

It should be noted that this place-where-*anything*-is-possible is quite powerful and should be treated with great care. If you are to think of going into this place within your mind you would *have to* feel completely safe and protected. After all, anything could be made true there, so you must be safe. A strong emphasis on safety and protection is needed when describing "the-place-where-anything-is-possible."

Here is an example of a script that describes "the place where anything is possible."

"...there is also a very special place within you...this is a place where anything can be made true...in this place you are completely safe...and you can try on new behaviors, new ideas, new beliefs and walk around with them and make them fit

before you ever take them into your real life...within this place where anything is possible you can safely do things...things you wouldn't tell even your closest friends...It is a place where only you can go...and when you feel right...you can bring with you those people...who understand this part of you...and together you can explore new feelings, new behaviors and new joys and pleasures...you have never dreamed of..."

This description gives respect to the power of this place and gives the subject full control to go there and bring others with him or her. If a hypnotist were to seal off this place-where-anything-is-possible then "bad things" are likely to occur. The hypnotist would soon become the whole source of pleasure to the subject and they would hounded to no end.

It is much wiser to give control of this place-where-anything-is-possible over to the subject and place yourself, the hypnotist, as an occasional welcomed guest.

The Test For The Place Where *Anything* Is Possible

To test this it's a good idea to start with something that is only *slightly* outside their normal behavior. For this this example I'll use public speaking.

"Go to that place where anything is possible and when you're there simply nod your head. (wait) Now see yourself at a distance speaking in public , confident , comfortable, completely at ease and

doing it with complete enjoyment. When you have that simply nod your head. (wait) *Good! Now feel that ease and confidence as you now step into your body and look through your eyes and feel the excitement and warmth of the people eager to hear your words. When you notice that feeling of confidence just nod your head."*

You'll notice that this was done is steps, first creating the new behavior and seeing it dissociated, from a distance, then associating into it only after all the positive feelings were described.

The Place of Forgetting

The place of forgetting is occasionally useful if the subject might have a tendency to over think a suggestion. If this is the case the suggestion is given and then the memory of the suggestion is cast into the-place-of-forgetting.

Here is one script that can help describe the place-of-forgetting.

"There is a place far far in the back of your mind. It is a place where you've put things that don't even matter...the phone numbers you've dialed only once, the names of people you've never met a second time...and back there things go that are no longer important...you'll find way back in the dark corners where you've forgotten so many things is a small black box that is filled with a vast emptiness...and if you put anything there is will simply fall away...and it no longer even matters...it's no longer important...gone...this is the place of forgetting."

Mind Control Hypnosis

You'll notice that this place of forgetting is the same "black box" that is mentioned in the initial hypnotic induction, so there should be some familiarity with it. This description simply adds more depth

The Test For The Place of Forgetting

The testing for this has been know to put off many neophyte hypnotists because it goes against reason that it should work. To those hypnotists I can only encourage you to be fearless and remember that you have asked the subjects to follow your suggestions *exactly,* and they have agreed.

The test would go as follows:

"...to show you the power of this place of forgetting...just for this moment...take your name and everything that has to do with your name and seal it...just for this moment...in that black box...seal tighter that you sealed your eyes closed just a moment ago...so that...as you walk away notice what happens when you, go ahead and try in vain to find the name and it's just not there...forgotten...when you notice that simply simply nod your head (wait) and let the box open and retrieve your name. You can leave anything you don't want in there..."

Here you have further tested the "black box" that is mentioned in the initial hypnotic induction. The hypnotist can further get feedback on his test by bringing the subject to the eyes open state and asking them to describe what they experienced when the sealed their name (Simply ask them "What was your experience when you sealed your name away?") The subject's experience can vary from simply not finding the name and being confused, to knowing their name but not trying to look for it. Regardless of what the subject experienced assure them they they did well and that hypnosis is a skill they learn and they will learn even more as they continue.

Mind Control Hypnosis

The Hypnotic Seal

The purpose of a hypnotic seal is to prevent anyone other than the programmer/hypnotist from accessing certain hypnotic states.

The hypnotic seal typically falls under the category of "a bad thing" for the simple reason that you prevent the subject from accessing useful mental/emotional states without the hypnotist. In theory it is easy to break a hypnotic seal, but it has been used by hypnotists who want the practice of hypnosis to be isolated only to doctors and people in the field of psychology.

Another type of seal would be "Anyone can hypnotize you but only I can bring you in and out of this particular state."

Applying the Hypnotic Seal:

1. Achieve true somnambulism.
2. Make the idea of a seal appealing, then obtain your client's consent.
3. Apply the type of seal that you want.
4. Give him amnesia for the entire conversation but reinforce the idea that the suggestion will work, even though he does not consciously remember anything about it.
5. Bring him up, question him to determine if he has amnesia. It is important while questioning not to mention anything about a seal.

Breaking the Hypnotic Seal:

Type 1a:
You may suspect a seal has been placed if your

subject does not respond to any of your suggestions, does not understand anything you are saying, or keeps popping out of hypnosis every time you obtain eye closure. *It is important that you never mention anything about the seal in your client's presence. Mention of the seal merely reinforces it.* The wording might be as follows:

"Someone has talked to you before about relaxation or hypnosis, is that right?...Can you visualize that person in your mind?...Maybe you can get a better picture of him with your eyes closed...Did he ever say in his conversation that your eyes are so relaxed or so heavy they won't work? (client says 'yes') Hear that voice in your mind...Hear him saying your eyes are so relaxed and so heavy they won't work...Do you hear his voice?... (client says 'yes') And they won't work — test them and see. Now you have perfect eye closure and the seal is broken."

Type 1b

Your client fails to respond to your suggestions because he or she does not understand what you are saying...it sounds like gibberish or a foreign language. To break the seal follow the same procedure as above but through an intermediary (third party).

Type 1c

Your client was told any other hypnotist attempting to hypnotize him would immediately become invisible and silent. Your client would not be able to see nor hear you. Break this type of seal by following the same procedure as above, using an intermediary.

Type 2

This is the easiest to break, for the person offers no objection to going into hypnosis. Let your client remain in hypnosis for a few minutes then bring him up. By taking your suggestion to come out of hypnosis, he has negated the seal of the original hypnotist.

Merely induce hypnosis again and explain what has transpired. Should the person interpret the seal as if it would not allow any other hypnotist to bring him or her out of hypnosis, proceed to treat it as the third type of seal.

Type 3

You may suspect this type of seal has been placed when usual and refractory methods for bringing your client out of hypnosis fail. The procedure is similar to the first type.
Say to your client:

"Picture the person who hypnotized you before and hear him saying those same words...To open your eyes and be totally alert...And they are beginning to open — your eyes are opening...All the way up now, totally alert, totally aware..."

Instructions for Hypnotic Seal Type 1c

If this Seal is present you must obtain someone

Mind Control Hypnosis

and train as an intermediary to assist you in case this ever occurs.

The intermediary that you choose to help out in this situation must not be a trained hypnotist. All they need to do is read the instructions or commit the instructions to memory. If they are trained as a hypnotist this will not work.

Instructions that your intermediary will need

Ask my client the following questions:

1. (Client's name), have you felt very relaxed before possibly in the presence of another person.
2. (Client's name), can you recall how you felt at that time.
3. (Client's name), did anyone help or teach you how to achieve that relaxation?

Now say to my client:

1. If you close your eyes maybe you can recall what was said to you.
2. Maybe you can think better with your eyes closed.
3. Imagine in your mind that you are hearing those same old instructions on how to relax.
4. Now you can hear the exact words that were said to you then. You can even remember how the voice sounded.
5. Can hear that voice in your mind?
6. Just imagine that he can hear that voice.
7. There was a time, when you were so relaxed your eyes wouldn't open...Remember how the

voice said to you… "and now your eyes are locked and won't open"…

When my client tries to open his or her eyes and fails, say the following:

"What has happened to you is based on a false belief that someone can entirely suggest away a person's suggestibility…This fallacy should be apparent since you have been following all my suggestions. Now, if such a thing were possible, the person would truly be a zombie…We know this does not occur in hypnosis because the human mind won't let it happen…A person can have a particular thought blocked off, however…This does not mean that the balance of the person's mind is kept from working. Since you now realize this…That effect that you have been displaying is now null and void…From this moment forward you will accept the suggestions which my colleague gives you that are good for you freely…My colleague will now be speaking to you and you will follow their instructions and suggestions…"

Hypnotic seals can take many forms, including the following:

- Simple hypnotic states that only the hypnotist can help the subject enter. *"You are now with me and in this state. Only when you are with me can you go into this state. Anyone else who makes suggestions for you to enter this state will automatically cause you to awaken with a shock…"*

Mind Control Hypnosis

- Direct suggestions for anxiety. *"If anyone other than me suggests you close your eyes and relax you will immediately become anxious. The more they encourage you the more anxious you will become. Only when I ask you will you follow and relax even deeper."*

- Suggesting that the subject will only understand the hypnotist. All other people are confusing and unintelligible. *"When anyone other than me asks you to enter this state you will notice they are not speaking your language. It will be very confusing. You will not understand them."*

- Suggesting that if the subject suspects a hypnotic suggestion is being made by anyone other than the hypnotist they must first gain approval from the hypnotist.

- By making the access to hypnotic states complex

Mind Control Hypnosis

Creating Useful Mental Structures In The Mind

What follows is an advanced way of helping someone to organize their mind. If this were your first introduction to hypnosis then this section will probably be a bit "out there" because it speaks of creating things within the mind as if they were real three dimensional objects. That said there is something of great use and benefit to building these processes.

If we can create useful metaphors for mental processes then, in hypnosis, the metaphors *become* the processes. This can then make change a much simpler accomplishment than most people think.

Let's start by proposing that one of the most beneficial values anyone can take on is flexibility. If one is flexible it means they can adapt to situations and events easily and they can build, find, and create resources at times when none previously existed. Taking it a step further, one can build even more wonderful feelings than they previously had. If you were to list all the good feelings it would not matter how long the list is ... it is not long enough. By using these mental constructs you can build within yourself and in others more of the flexibility that will create the ultimate freedom people desire.

Remembering that when you name something it becomes real and when you describe it it comes alive, you can now go from creating places in the mind to create constructs that have a predetermined purpose. These constructs can have shape, size, color and dimension that help designate their purpose, but they are wholly mental creations in the subjects mind.

How this is applied is only as limited as the

Mind Control Hypnosis

creativeness of the operator. The subject and operator together can create entire mental and emotional mindscapes complete with all the mental structures needed for the most effective life experience.

What follows are examples of how the subject can be trained to "see" this construct, and then examples of their application.

Training to Hallucinate

The subject is told that they will learn how to create powerful and useful mental tools and shown how to enhance their minds ability to visualize. The first step is done in a non-hypnotized state.

They are first shown an ordinary object that has minimal details. It could be a simple black box or a ketchup bottle. They are told to look at it with their full attention and memorize it. Next they are told to close their eyes and imagine it in their mind. The object is then removed and they open their eyes. They are asked if the object is present. They answer no. Then, they are asked if they can still see the object in their mind. When the answer is "yes," as it usually is, they proceed to the next step.

With their eyes open the are asked to imagine a turntable with the object in the center of it. They are to focus their eyes where that imaginary object would be on that imaginary turntable. Once they have done that they are told to reach out with their finger and touch the edge of the turntable to slowly rotate the object. They are asked if they can see the objects different sides as they rotate the turntable. This step begins to link their kinesthetic/feeling modality to their visual modality and for those who have not experienced this before they will actually "see" the object and may be locked in fascination at their new found ability.

The next step is to enhance that ability by having the subject do it while in hypnosis.

"...Now with your eyes closed see the object on the turn table and just as before, reach out with your hand and rotate it and tell me when you can see it's other sides...now put your hand down and do the same process entirely in your mind...watching the object rotate at the speed you determine...and tell me when you can see it's other sides."

Using this method any mental construct can be made.

Water

Water is a very useful mental construct when something needs to be "washed away" like pain or anxiety. This can be tested if the subject has a pain or headache.

Jewels, Gems and Crystals

Jewels, gems and crystals themselves have a certain romance, glamor and appeal. As objects within the imagination they can be used to radiate a specific mental or emotional state. They can also be used as markers that designate a certain part of the subject's mental journey.

Mind Control Hypnosis

Bottles, Boxes, Treasure Chests and Containers

Containers are mental constructs that are used to hold things. These things could be resources, abilities, information or emotions.

As containers these mental constructs can take any form; boxes, bottles, jars, cans. In many ways containers are like rooms, which are mentioned below. The differences between containers and rooms are that you can enter a room but you cannot enter a container. Another difference is that resources/abilities/information etc. are created prior to the introducing the container. Using rooms the resources are usually created within the room and thus further distanced from the conscious mind.

"You take all of your fear of not being creative and put them into a bottle. The bottle now becomes a bundle of energy. Now imagine you are opening the bottle and out of the sack comes a rainbow of energy. It is powerful, it is positive. You are now full of new ideas. You can feel this power surge through your body. Your mind is now clear and focused. You feel confident, sure of your talent and eager to set your new ideas into motion, and you control the energy in your life. You are very successful in controlling the energy in your life. You take a few breaths and relax. You notice the neighborhood around you. There is a beautiful park. You begin to notice how beautiful the day is, and you begin to feel a fresh new energy flowing through your body...the more calm you become the more enthusiastic and creative you become...you will feel free to create, to enjoy your creative talent, to invent, to shape, and form new and wonderful ideas."

Rotating Objects

Because of the sensory confusion that can be created by spinning, objects that spin can be useful anchors to trigger amnesia or to lock away suggestions from the conscious mind.

"...imagine a black box...and in this black box place all your memories of these suggestions so that they will rest comfortably in there allowing you to carry them out without ever having to think of them...now seal the box up and watch it begin to spin...slowly at first...so that you can see it's other sides, and with each full rotation it turns ever so much faster. Turning and turning and turning...and it will remain turning and turning, forever turning in your mind."

Of course you are not limited to black boxes. Anything that spins can be used. Music boxes with a spinning ballerina inside are a common experience for many people and can useful.

Looped or Figure 8 type Objects

Objects that are looped can be figure eights, infinity signs, mobius strips, etc. can also be useful mental constructs.

These shapes have two immediate applications. They can be "loops" that stick people into a specific state. They can also be used as a "reset" that brings someone back to an original state when distracted.

The "loop" construct would have two emotions

on either side of the figure eight and the subject would follow the line of the loop going from one state to the next back and forth ad infinitum.

"Imagine now a figure eight or infinity sign and you'll see how the line moves so fluidly from one side, curving around to the next. On one side I want you to put the feeling of pleasure there so that you focus on that half of the figure eight you feel pleasure, and on the other side of the figure eight you feel acceptance...begin now to carefully follow the line as it curves on one side generating for you pleasure and on the other side acceptance...going back and forth from one state to the next and notice how well the fit together one after another. Just go back and forth enjoying this process. (pause) Now place this figure eight there in the back of your mind where a part of you can focus on it as the rest of you hears and follows each suggestion...and if your mind wanders away you can always return it to the figure eight and the cycle of pleasure and acceptance."

To use the loop as a "reset" allows the cycle to be broken up so not to repeat. Then the process with this break is repeated until it is ingrained as a response.

"...imagine now a figure eight or infinity sign and you'll see how the line moves so fluidly from one side, curving around to the next. On one side you can see mental clarity, calmness of mind...on the other side is fear and anxiety...Begin now to focus on the line of the figure eight that is on the anxiety side so that as you follow it you can feel that discomfort and anxiety. When you move to the other

side of the figure eight you immediately feel the calmness of mind and mental clarity...when you notice that calmness, nod your head."

The operator waits for a response. As soon as the subject reports calm the operator continues) *Notice the calm and open your eyes to feel that calm.* Other versions of "breaks" can be "move your head around," "shake your hands and arms, etc. This process is then practiced until the response becomes automatic. It is a constant process of rehearse and test, rehearse and test, towards an automatic response.

Walls, Doors, and Barriers

Walls, doors, and barriers are useful constructs when there are things that require being hidden from the conscious awareness of the subject. Keep in mind that archetypal symbolism of a door represents change or transition to a new state. Within that state can be placed information or behaviors that would be outside the subject's awareness.

The first step is to create the door and give it a key. Upon opening the door with the key and entering a mental state is created within the room with all the associated visual, auditory, and kinesthetic experiences. Only then is the information or behavior implanted. For example:

"Now you will see a door. The door is large and black with yellow polka dots. When you reach to open the door you notice that it is locked. No matter how hard you try it will not open because the door

needs a key. I will give you the key and I alone will hold the key. The key is a word (or shape, or sound.) The key is my voice alone saying _____, and upon me and me alone saying the key _____ the door opens. Now you can easily step inside beyond the door and there is a large and beautiful room. The room is dimly lit, and within it are floating beautiful yellow orbs providing light where ever they go...there is within this room a lightness as if gravity is only one fifth of normal, and a pleasant joy...when you now notice those feelings simply nod your head...and the next wonderful step will follow... (wait)...now you will receive the information that is only available within this room behind the black door with yellow polka dots..." (The information is given and then asked to be repeated and tested until the answer is returned automatically.)

Keys can also be events and situations so that "when X occurs the door will open and you will do Y (or have the information)..."
The best way to do this is through the process of training and testing, training and testing.

The Delta and The Delta State

The Delta is a symbol that is used to represent "the difference that makes all the difference." In mathematics it is used to represent a quality of change. In marketing Delta represents the factor that sets a product apart from it's competitors.
The purpose of the Delta state is to create a template from which anything can be created. In the Delta state the subject is a blank slate, upon which anything can be created. One of the most effective

ways to do that is to suggest a mental state that has no reference point; a place that is outside of time, space and dimension. The Delta state is unique and must be tested and validated for amnesia and for the ease of creating harmless arbitrary mental constructs like mental lenses that only sees things in black and white, or an eye patch that causes temporary blindness in one eye.

First you take the subject through the regular induction and testing for somnambulism:

"Now let all the awareness fade away so that you can now find yourself in a safe place where there is no color or light or dark...when you have that place simply nod your head. (pause) Now take away all sensation and awareness of time and gravity...all gone...and after you've done that you'll find you are safe and completely ready to proceed. When you have done that simply nod your head."

It should be noted that numerous objects, figure eights, doors, and Deltas can be made and distinguished from one another by making them different colors and sizes, and each can have it's separate function.

To accommodate the individuality of the subject the operator/hypnotist can give the subject a survey asking, "When you feel satisfaction (or any emotion) what color do you envision it to be?" and "When you feel (name an emotion) what body sensation do you best associate with that emotion?" The survey will yield a list of emotions, associated colors, and body sensations. With the information received from the subject the operator can then make mental constructs that better fit the subject.

Mind Control Hypnosis

So if the subject experiences "pleasure" as pink and the bodily sensation as "tingly" the operator can suggest a "pleasure room" for example, with a pink door and upon entering the subject feels a tingly sensation.

By the time the hypnotists begins using these mental constructs they have a certain leeway that allows them to make the hypnosis appear more magical. Remember what was stated at the beginning of this course, that while people are told hypnosis is not magic, they want magic to happen. Here the hypnotist can begin to give seemingly magical names to the constructs and processes through which they guide the subject. Those names play to the subjects hidden desire for a magical experience.

Unconscious Mental Structures and Machines

Remembering that "when you name something it becomes real, and when you describe it it comes alive" one can create "things" or "machines" in the mind that serve a useful function while working at an unconscious level.

Perhaps you've known people who can awaken from sleep at a predetermined time without the aid of an alarm clock. This is because they have created a mental alarm clock that is there to help them.

In the hypnosis session the process is to first name the form by saying what it will do, and then describe how it will do it. Because people learn best from a meaningful experience the hypnotist would then have the subject go through the experience of the "mind machine" working. This would be repeated until the subject gets a consistent response with no conscious effort.

When creating a "mind machine" for the first time it's a good idea to emphasize the importance of calibrating the machine. Using the alarm clock as an example, for the first few attempts, the subject may not awaken at the right time, maybe awakening too early or too late. These are not to be regarded as failures but as calibration points to reset the alarm.

Mind machines can also be thought of as types of computer programs because they tend to follow an "if/then" procedural process (example: *"If it's 6:00am then I awaken"*) .

Mind machines can take many forms but they will tend to fall into these categories:

Assisting Machines

Assisting machines unconsciously help the subject to organize information and give instructions on how to proceed.

Alerts and Alarms

Alerts point out opportunities to the subject when they become available.

An alert could automatically make you aware of possible money making opportunities, or perhaps when attractive romantic partners are within sight. An example of this would be what's referred to as "gay-dar" within the gay community.

Alarms are designed to make you aware when a possible threat is near. People who spent time amid abusive alcoholics are often able to quickly recognize people with drug dependency issues.

Mind Control Hypnosis

Defensive Devices

Defensive machines are an offshoot of alarms that automatically begin behaviors to keep the subject safe. An if/then example of an automatic defensive device would be "If I'm alone in an unfamiliar environment then I become very aware of all the people around me."

Well trained body guards have create very strong defensive mind machines to keep them and their clients safe.

Influencing Machines

Influencing machines are used when dealing directly with other people for the purposes of influencing them.

Influencing machines automatically bring together a combination of sharp observation, learned skilled and focused desires to keep the subject focused on persuading others to their goals.

Some sales people simply think of it as a "switch" that they turn on and it brings to bare all of their skills and talents right when they need them.

Mind Control Hypnosis

Useful Hypnosis Scripts

What follows are various hypnosis processes that can be of use in helping people overcome personal limitations such as fears and compulsive habits.

The Mirror of The Future
(While he may humbly deny it I would like to credit hypnotist, Jeff Stephens, for this script).

When working with people for therapeutic reasons one of the greatest obstacles to overcome is the subject's own lack of self worth, self esteem, and deservingness. Often the subject has a personal history filled with attempts and subsequent failures that effect even their willingness to try any further. They often approach hypnosis as a final attempt and are already disheartened and desperate.

When working with people for weight loss I will often propose a thought experiment in which I ask the subject to pretend that they are actually an identical twin separated at birth. Upon finally meeting their twin they both realize they need to lose the same amount of weight, and they both set out to do it.

At the end a certain period of time they both are successful. Both lost the same weight over the same time doing the same activities. The only difference is that one of them lost weight because they hated themselves and the other did it because they loved themselves. The story ends by asking them which twin would they rather be?

The purpose of the *The Mirror of The Future* is to rebuild the self image so that they proceed with purpose and commitment.

"In a moment I will count back from five to zero, and as I do you will go further into that deep and pleasant state. Imagine that there is a zero out there in front of you, and with each count you get closer, finally going through that zero, inside that zero and the all the way down into that zero. From that point on every word you hear can be made absolutely true allowing you to change in all the ways you've always wanted to change for so long."

"5...4...3...2...1...Zero. FORGET...trust your unconscious mind to do it's perfect work...and notice that you can see yourself in the mirror. From this point on when you look in the mirror you LIKE what you see in the mirror."

"I'm speaking directly to the unconscious mind ...so the conscious mind can just drift away in whatever direction you like, or it can stay and pay attention to each and every word as you go deeper and deeper inside."

"From this point on you LIKE what you see in the mirror. From this point on you LIKE that person you see in the mirror. From this point on you LIKE yourself."

"Unconscious mind, you like (name) and from this point on you like, love and DEEPLY accept (name) and because you want to make him/her happy you do EVERYTHING necessary to make (name) happy and healthy. From this point on you like what you see in the mirror, you like (name) and no longer do you see what you had seen in the past. No longer do you focus on the pain, bitterness and failure. No longer do you see the (name) that was, the (name) that had to be. From this point on when you look in the mirror you see the (name) that CAN be. You see the (name) that WILL be...you see the (name) that IS going to be...for the (name) that WILL BE...IS the (name) that exists right now...and you do EVERYTHING in your power to make THAT (name) happen. You do EVERYTHING necessary to make (name) healthy – Financially, Spiritually, Emotionally, Relationally and Physically. Those five areas of health are from now on THE MOST important thing to you without exception."

"You release all sabotage. You have no need to struggle any longer because you're done. You're done with the bitterness the hurt and the failure. You're done with any need to punish yourself or to feel guilt or shame. You are done with ALL of that...FOREVER."

"You like yourself from now on and and you let go of any need to notice criticism from other people or even yourself."

"You let go of all self criticism because from this point forward you like yourself and have no need for it any longer."

"(Name), if I throw a dart at a wall, it will damage the wall and if I throw it a window the window will shatter...But if I throw it as a river it doesn't damage the water because the river does not make a wall out of itself, and you are no longer making a wall out of yourself any longer either. You no longer make walls out of your self because you realize that by being that river you cannot be damaged by the darts of criticism. You no longer need to worry about the darts of criticism any longer because you have let go of the need to notice criticism from others and even from yourself."

"From now on, you are done with self-

sabotage in every way. You are done with any sabotage of yourself."

"You feel good about yourself from the INSIDE now. Your river flows from the spring within you so your self esteem comes from the INSIDE now. What other people think and say does not matter. If there is a lesson you need to learn you learn it without feeling bad and you can learn any lesson and it will not hurt your feelings. You simply use EVERYTHING to improve your health...financially, relationally, emotionally and physically."

"From this point on you're DONE with failure and you focus ONLY on the future. That is THE most important thing from this point on."

This script has been know to bring tears to subjects eyes because for many this is often the first time they were told that they could feel good about themselves for no reason.

The Cravings Crusher

This is a technique I've made from a modified anchor collapse. It is designed to eliminate or minimize cravings and desire.

The Cravings Crusher was first tried on weight loss clients for chocolate and chips and was later incorporated for smokers.

To begin I ask *"do you have cravings?"* Many people will easily say "yes," but others may need a further explanation. *"A craving is when you have a thought to eat something, and that thought won't go away until you're satisfy it."*

Then ask them, *"if you thought about it could you bring up a craving right now?"* This is important for the process to work and most people will say yes. If they say no, or "I don't know" then encourage them to try and remind them that for the the process to work well they need to bring up a craving.

"Here is what is going to happen. I'm going to ask you to sit with your hand resting either on your lap or the arms of the chair palm up. You'll be looking into the palms of your hand. When you look into your right hand I want you to bring up a craving. In you left hand I want to imagine being completely free of cravings, at your ideal weight (a non-smoker) and feeling great! At some point I'm going to have you bring your hands together and it is going to get very confusing so just follow along with me. OK?"

In the hundreds of times I've done this I never had anyone ask anything more about the process. Begin the process as follows:

Mind Control Hypnosis

"Okay, sit with your hands resting comfortably either on the arms of the chair or on you lap. Look in to you right hand. As you focus intently on the right hand I want you to bring up a craving. When you notice that craving...simply nod your head. Take your time. (wait for response) Good! Now as you notice that craving focus on the feeling of the craving. It's not about the food/smoking. It's about the feeling of the craving and imagine that craving is in the right hand. Either you're holding that craving or that's where it originates but that craving is in the right hand."

"Take a deep breath...and look into the left hand. As you look into the left hand...imagine that you are completely free from cravings. You're looking through your own eyes at your ideal weight/a non-smoker, you're feeling fine, in perfect health. When you notice that incredible feeling and all the wonderful resources you have simply nod your head (wait for response.) Good!"

"Now, turn to your right hand and notice the craving. (wait for response). Now, turn to you left and notice all those wonderful resources there waiting for you...and close your eyes...and I want you to SLOWLY bring those hands together as if they're being pulled together by an magnetic force...and soon they will come together...and those two feelings will crash and collide and smash together...it will be very confusing...but that confusion will pass...so let them come together (wait until the hands meet)...and when that confusion passes you'll know it...because you'll feel fine...so let those two feelings mix, merge and intertwine and when the confusion has passed nod your head (wait *for response.)"*

"Now, I'm going to ask you a question and I want you to tell me...what happens...now...when you go ahead and try in vane to bring up a craving...what do you notice? (Wait for response. They will typically report that they cannot bring up a craving or that it's drastically minimized.)"

"That's right. Notice that response. So now imagine taking any last minimal remnant of the craving and tossing it behind and it just begins to fall away...it doesn't even matter. It isn't even important. You don't even have to do a thing about it. Gone...and notice that incredible feeling of relief."

"Now imagine yourself, today, tonight or tomorrow when you would have normally had this craving but NOW you have this response. As soon as you notice it you take the very thought of a craving and you toss it behind you where it doesn't even matter...and feel that relief."

"Now just create one event right after another where you already have this response. Different places, different times and this response is already there. Again and again and again and again. (pause, give them time to do this for a while)"

"So when you notice...NOW...that you can't even bring up a craving no matter how hard you try...what sort of thoughts and feeling come up? (They usually will mention a positive feeling like "relief"or "control." If they say something that is other than clearly positive then guide them to a positive feeling.) Good! Notice that relief. Focus in on it and say this loudly within you mind...and feel it in your heart...hear yourself say, "I deserve this. I deserve this. I deserve this." You do deserve this feeling of relief."

Mind Control Hypnosis

The next step is to have them open their eyes and notice what it's like to be free from cravings. Most people will not be able to bring up a craving no matter how hard they try.

The nature of this process is similar to an NLP anchor collapse when two opposing feeling are brought together. These two feelings cannot coexist at the same time thus creating a temporary feeling of confusion. But the mind sorts it out because the mind cannot easily maintain a constant state of confusion.

Once the subject has an experience of NOT having a craving they are taught a useful response to cravings, one of tossing it behind them. This is follow by rehearsing the process until it becomes unconscious and automatic.

The concept of "Deserving" is introduced to help the subject at the level of their self-worth and personal identity, and is sometimes the most powerful part of the process.

This process is often done just preceding the "hypnosis" process because it is not entirely like what people think of hypnosis. Usually because of the dramatic effect it has on the subject it encourages the subject to be more comfortable complying to the suggestions during the hypnosis that follows.

The Cravings Crusher also provide an example of how to "throw something behind you and let it go," which is a useful process to learn when you want to change old behaviors.

Mind Control Hypnosis

Creating Negative Hallucinations

Ever since Bob saw the fire that destroyed his house he cringes at the sight of flame and fire. The anxiety has kept him of visiting his friends, most of whom smoke. Now even a match or a lighter seems as big as fireplace. He even sees it when it is not there.

What bob sees at times can be called a hallucination.

A hallucination is when something is seen though nothing is there. A negative hallucination is the opposite, where you don't see something that is there.

Negative hallucinations are very useful and helpful when it comes to removing things that are either unpleasant or emotional triggers.

There are several ways to create a negative hallucination. If you've read my book *Mind Control Language Patterns* you'll discover a few helpful hints in the section called *"The Book of Forgetting.'* The way to create a negative hallucination using hypnosis is through direct suggestion and minimization.

The normal testing for amnesia is needed. The direct suggestions can be: *"the fire is not here. As if it were blank...meaningless..."*

You can begin these suggestions by linking pleasant feelings to the process of removing the image:

"... from a distance see a picture on a wall. The picture has a frame around it and the picture is that of a fire (or whatever you want to negatively hallucinate.) Now erase the fire and feel the

relief...as you paint over it notice the joy...and continue to erase it from your mind...the more you continue to clear it away the more joy and pleasure you feel. You have now a constant process of removing...erasing...and wiping away all the thoughts, responses and images about that...forget...completely just let it fall from your mind...and just notice the joy and pleasure that is left behind."

The minimization suggestions are designed to tell the mind how to perceive what is bothering them. Minimizing suggestions will sound like:

"... make is smaller and smaller...push it far away... let all the color just flow from it...as if nothing is there...and let it fall far far behind you...where it doesn't even matter...it's no longer important...gone...you don't even have to think about it...and you mind does this...right now and every time you're in it's presence...and under these circumstances...your mind will just shrink it away...tiny tiny tiny...like a dot that just falls away... your mind does this every time...like it's doing now...again and again..."

To personally test the effectiveness of this imagine a hamburger, or your favorite most delicious distraction, and go through the process of imagining it shrunk down, pushed away, turned black and white and move it away, all in your mind, of course, and notice how it's appeal has changed.

Make it a habit every time you see or think of your delicious distraction and notice how you respond differently to it.

Mind Control Hypnosis

To do this in hypnosis and make it an unconscious reaction is merely a matter of practicing the response in hypnosis until it becomes easy, testing it several times. When it becomes automatic in hypnosis then test it during the waking state, out of hypnosis.

Mind Control Hypnosis

The NLP Phobia Hypnosis Process

When someone reports they have a phobia they want to get rid of there are some very effect and rapid ways to do it using hypnosis and NLP processes. The hypnosis process that follows is one that I use that dramatically reduces the subject's fear and anxiety.

The first step is to, in a matter of fact way, introduce the NLP phobia cure process as a "test." You would say, *"I just want to have you go through a very quick process to see how you respond. This is not a pass/fail type of test. I use it so that I can more easily modify the hypnosis process to fit your needs."* You say this to make sure that they are getting a useful response, but framing it so that they are not under any pressure to perform.

It should be noted that this short "test" is often all that is needed to remove a phobia. It is placed here to give the subject momentum to continue through the hypnosis process and create an even more powerful hypnosis process.

Let's assume the subject has a fear of dogs that prevents her from strolling the neighborhood with her family.

"First, Can you think of the last time you were frightened by a dog? Think about that now and what sort of feelings are you feeling as you think about it?"

The purpose of this line of questioning is to get a base line to compare to when the hypnosis session is over.

"And even when you try to relax and calm yourself are you still anxious?" This question too is part of the base line.

Mind Control Hypnosis

"Okay. Before we do the hypnosis let me just walk you through this very quickly. Follow along with me as fast as you can. Don't analyze or judge what's happening, just imagine it in your mind as quickly as I describe it. I'll also ask you to occasionally nod your head. Are you ready?"

As you do this process the goal is to speak just fast enough that the subject will only have enough time to keep up with you. This doesn't have to be a machine gun delivery, just one with a minimum of pauses.

"Close your eyes and imagine yourself in a very comfortable chair in a big beautiful movie theater. You can see on the movie screen an image of yourself relaxed and comfortable. From that seat lift up out of your body and float up...up...back...to the projection room...and from that projection room grab the reel of film that shows your most recent experience...except that this reel of film will show you reacting calmly and undisturbed just as you've seen others so easily respond in that situation. Now let the movie move forward in time to that time when, no matter what, you are ok with dogs (or whatever their fear) and you're standing there feeling absolutely wonderful, and when you are there simply nod your head...take all the time you need (wait.)"

"Great! Now jump into the screen and be there looking through your eyes at that time in the future and feeling through your senses at ease and comfortable...now imagine the film being played in reverse as fast as you can with you in it...doing *everything backwards...until you're right back to this moment in time...right here...right now...going backwards, and when you're back here to this moment just nod your head (wait.)"*

As soon as the subject is back ask them, *"now, when you think about that incident with the dog (or the fear) what do you notice that is different?"*

The subject will usually report that they no longer have fear or anxiety when they rethink the event.

It should be noted that often this one very rapid "test" is enough to eliminate a long time phobia. Many NLPers would simply stop there. The reason I recommend that you proceed quickly to the hypnosis is to give them their money's worth and create a more powerful experience.

When the subjects report that they are remembering the event without anxiety, the typical response is *"You did great. Notice how it's not there even now. Let's do the hypnosis."*

Following the hypnotic induction the hypnotist would go through the same process. The main difference is that it will be repeated several times within the hypnosis session, and with each repetition a new resource is added each time and in different situations. The subject is encouraged to go through each process completely, and as quickly as is manageable.

Without writing out the entire hypnotic script and it's repetitions, an outline of the process is as follows:

1. You are resting in a comfortable movie theater seat. In front of you is a black and white image

of yourself just as you are now resting comfortably.
2. You float out of your body up and back to the movie projection room.
3. You put a reel of film in the projector that is about you doing the action perfectly and without fear, each time adding a new positive resource.
4. From the projection room you watch the movie play all the way to the end when you are free of fear or anxiety.
5. You jump into the movie and experience those feelings in the first person as if you are there.
6. The movie runs quickly backward until you roll the movie back to the moment just before the event.

Once the subject has done this enough times to know how the process works the hypnotist can tell the subject to repeat the process on their own.

During sessions like this I have at times told the subject:

"Do this same process rapidly again and again until you feel that you've already done it 100 times in you mind without counting. You go through the process repeating it quickly again and again until it's ingrained within you. Take all the time you need until that feeling is right, that you've already done it 100 times without even counting, and when you're there simply nod your head."

By doing it this way the subjects tend to count 100 repetitions unconsciously and involve themselves more deeply in the process.

Mind Control Hypnosis

For Fun: Hypnotic Drunkenness

If a person wants to give a dramatic public demonstration of hypnosis and make it fun then hypnotic drunkenness will do it.

In short, hypnotic drunkenness is simply using hypnosis to create the feeling of being drunk in someone. For the people who volunteer to be the subject it's incredible fun, and for those watching it's a huge laugh.

Because of the overall fun and pleasure of this effect I'll describe in a step-by-step format how to do it.

Step 1. Select The Right Candidate

It's best to enlist someone who considers themselves to be a "fun drunk," meaning they giggle when intoxicated with alcohol. You can start by simply asking if there is anyone in the audience who knows they get "silly" when drunk. It's likely you'll find some eager volunteers, especially if the audience is of college age. Remind everyone that whole experience is designed to be fun.

Step 2. Get Agreement From Your Volunteer and Begin to Elicit Their "Getting Drunk" Process

After your volunteer has agreed to follow your suggestions ask them to tell you the very first thing they notice as they drink *just before* they begin to get drunk, and beginning with their first sip of alcohol.

Continue to ask the question, "what do you notice or do next?" In so doing you're getting details of what they do internally as they get drunk. You may find there are three or four steps to this process, but there may be more. Take note of the steps.

Step 3. Go Through the Process

Ask your subject to close their eyes and begin to walk them through the steps just as they described them (without them taking in any alcohol, of course.) Make certain they bring about (or imagine) the sensations they would be feeling.

Step 4. Repeat

Repeat this several times. You may have to do it as many as 10 or 15 times, perhaps more. You'll know they are responding because they'll begin to act intoxicated and, because you screened them for it, they'll begin to get funny and giggly.

Step 5. Have Fun

This includes having them do all the normal tests for intoxication:

- Walking in a straight line
- Reciting the alphabet
- Extending arms to their sides and touching their nose
- Extending arms to their sides and standing on one foot

Mind Control Hypnosis

You can also see how their behavior is different in social settings by having them talk to other people, always good for a laugh.

Concluding The Demonstration

At the end of this demonstration it's always a good idea to make certain your subject leaves in the sober condition they started, so tell them "on the count of three I will clap my hands and you will return completely sober, alert, wide awake and feeling great. One. Two. Three (Clap!)"

Mind Control Hypnosis

The Dantalion Jones Hypnosis Setting

Among hypnotists and psychedelic drug users there is a saying, "set and setting are everything." What this means is that the ***where*** you're having the altered state is just as important as the altered state itself.

Hypnotists have a long tradition about what a hypnotist's office should look like.

It's often suggested that a hypnotist's office should have warm colors and a comfortable chair for the subject. Additionally, a background of new age music is often played to assure the subject is in a comfortable condition.

I am not one of those hypnotists.

I am in full agreement that set and setting are important, and I propose a radical change from what a traditional hypnotist's workspace might look like.

Please keep in mind that while I have reasons for what I will be suggesting, this is entirely personal. I am not proposing a radical change for every hypnotist's office, just a change in various ways we look at the hypnosis setting.

To get an understanding of why these changes are being suggested let's go back to the original paradox about people and hypnosis, namely, that people need to know that hypnosis is *nott* magical, yet have it presented in a way that helps them experience it as magical. Done correctly this will let them know that *they* are responsibility for their success, and bypass their conscious understanding so that their results are powerful and lasting.

In this ideal hypnosis setting there would be two rooms. One for the pre-talk and one for the hypnosis session. The pre-talk office is in every way normal, and designed to get the subject comfortable and bring them to the ultimate agreement to follow the hypnotist's suggestions as they've been described.

The mood in the pre-talk office should be lighthearted with a strong emphasis on being informative. Upon getting the agreement to follow the hypnotist's suggestion the hypnotist simply says, "great, let's get started," and stands and walks out with a gesture for the subject to follow.

The hypnosis room is a featureless room with a small circular table in the center and two straight backed wooden chairs on either side facing each other. The hypnotist sits in one chair and the subject in the other.

There are several reasons for this setup.

Reason 1

To defy the subject's expectations of what a hypnosis session should be like. After all, they have agreed to follow your suggestions and not judge, analyze or evaluate.

Reason 2

To add a minor bit of confusion as to what is to happen. The setting of two chairs and a table are innocuous and safe enough, but again a bit confusing. This helps to overload the sensory input of the subject.

Reason 3

With the table separating the hypnotist and subject they can easily place their hand on the table. This makes the subject's hands available for setting anchors. At the same time the table provides a boundary of safety.

Reason 4
With the hands accessible on the table the hypnotist can add to the sensory overload by a simple process of very gently tapping on back on the hands.

Reason 5
The setting allows the hypnotist to train the subject to follow their suggestions with simple commands like, "come on in," "have a seat," "no, take this one," "move closer," "put your hands here," "get comfortable," and so on.

I have fantasized of having the table and two chairs setup in the middle of a large dark basement with a single light dangling overhead. This may add a component of fear into the subject's experience (which I don't mind as long as they follow the suggestions), and thus contribute to the magical quality of the hypnosis experience. Sometimes all that is needed to create a feeling of the magical is a little sense of drama.

Mind Control Hypnosis

The PMC Processes

My first book, *Perfected Mind Control*, contained what I still feel are some of them most powerful hypnosis processes ever made public. Combine those processes with the insights I've written about here, and you are on your way to being a top-notch hypnotist with unimaginable power. For that reason I'm including a discussion of them in this book.

As someone who now has some skill and knowledge in hypnosis I ask you to read these hypnosis processes in a very unique and powerful way - read them as if you are doing them on yourself. In other words, put yourself in the position of the hypnotic subject and make all of these suggestion *real* for you. It is then that you will understand their power. It is then you will decide if you wish to proceed any further.

"It's dangerous to understand new things too quickly."
~Josiah Warren – *True Civilization*

I hope you haven't jumped to this section without reading everything that has preceded it. If you have, you're not ready. Go back. Start at the beginning and try, really try, to get an idea of this is all about, because what follows is what you as an operator will be using with your subject.

If you do it right, everyone you work with will love you. If you do it wrong...you'll pay for it in the long run.

Mind Control Hypnosis

The lesson is (yes, I'll say it again) *do these processes on yourself first!* Only then can you use them with the respect they deserve.

Mind Control Hypnosis

The "Creating An Inner Voice" Open Process

The purpose of an "open" process is that it can be inserted anytime during the other similar sessions. It's a very benevolent process that can get anyone to easily feel good about who they are and what you're doing with them. In the hypnosis world it does what is called "ego strengthening" for the subject. For that reason it's quite good for the subject's first introduction to the PMC processes.
Additionally, if the operator feels that the subject is not responding well or quickly enough then, no need to rush. Simply introduce this simple and enjoyable process that has many benefits.

Objectives:

• To build the subject's sense of comfort with the PMC processes in general.

• To build the subject's confidence.

• To build an enjoyable anticipation to learning about themselves, and changing to fit their wants and needs.

• To create an ongoing internal voice that will continue to provide positive and beneficial reinforcement to the subject on both a conscious and unconscious level.

• To covertly install the operator's voice as a nurturing voice within the subject's consciousness.
Please note as you read this that the suggestions given would be suggestions that we all

would like to hear. If these suggestions are an internal endless loop within our minds then we would each be much more likely to feel good about things, be more flexible to challenges, and be happy in general. I'm including the hypnotic induction in hopes that this will make things simpler.

You'll also notice that early on that the subject is being enlisted to not merely lay passively with eyes closed, but to engage in responses to the operator. This cannot be underestimated. Responsiveness Is Important!

The Induction

*You'll find that this only takes a very short amount of time for you... so ...   Take that moment and close your eyes... begin to become aware of the muscles of your forehead and let them ... **relax**... as the muscles of the forehead relaxes you can notice that the eyes and eye lids naturally... **remain closed**... so now focus on the eyes and eyelids and relax them even further and they will continue to ... **stay closed** ... let your eyes gently gaze now, beneath closed eyelids at the center of your forehead and in a voice within **your mind** tell the eyelids to... "Stay closed!". .. and if you like very briefly test them and stop and **go deeper...** which only means to **become more comfortable**... and you don't even have to move to do that. (PAUSE) ... once again tell the eyelids "Stay closed" and if you like briefly test them and stop testing and... **go deeper**... even more relaxed. More comfortable than you were even just a moment ago... and as you notice your degree of relaxation there are even greater levels of* relaxation which I call levels A, B and C and let me describe them to you before you actually **go there.**

When you go to Level A ... but don't go there yet ... you'll relax yourself even more than you are right now. And when you reach level A you'll easily be able to move the index finger of the right hand.

When you go to level B I want you to relax so much that it takes all your effort to move the index finger of the right hand... and you may only get just a small visible twitch because you're so relaxed.

Finally, when you go to level C I want you to imagine as if you've relaxed it **all** away so that even though you know that you're trying to move the index finger everything will ... **stay perfectly still.**

So when you're ready go to that level A. When you feel you are more relaxed than you were just a moment ago gently move the index finger of your right hand. (wait) Good! When you're ready relax even further... go to that level B... where you are so relaxed it takes all your will and effort to move the index finger... because you're so relaxed... you may only get a small motion or twitch enough for me to see. And even thought it's hard I know you can do it. (wait) Good!

Keep relaxing. **Go Deeper...** as if you have relaxed **everything** **away**... so relaxed that even though you know that you're trying to move the finger... everything stays... perfectly still. .. and you know you're safe. You're completely in control. And if something truly needed your attention you could easily emerge from this state... but now ... even though you know that you're trying to move the finger... everything stays... **perfectly still.**

From here there are four things that we can do whenever you're within this process state . The first is you can simply follow the suggestions and just by doing that you have already achieved a comfortably pleasant state of awareness. You've done very well.

The second thing we can do is I can ask you to imagine something and it can instantly come to mind. For example I'd like you to now imagine a crystal ball with a beautiful red rose inside of it.

The third thing is that I can mention feelings and you can become instantly aware of them. And because you are within this process state now you can notice how easy it is. From now on you don't even have to try your mind will **notice this automatically**. For example even though you might not have been aware of it a moment ago because you are in this pleasant state you can automatically become aware of the shoes on your feet. You might notice the feel or the weight on comfort of discomfort. And even though you haven't been thinking about it you can notice the feeling of your hands resting comfortably where they are right now. You may notice the pressure or texture or the temperature. And you can also notice the feeling of the surface beneath you giving you complete support enough to **relax even more comfortably** with every word.

The forth thing we can do is I can ask you to recall memories and they can instantly come to you. I will ask you to remember only pleasant memories. When you recall these pleasant memories I'd like *you let me know by moving the right index finger. (wait) Good!*

And now I'd like you to recall a pleasant memory of you around a swing. It could be your swing or the a friends swing or swing at a park or play ground. When that pleasant memory comes to mind move your right index finger. (wait) Good!

*And I'd like to remember a time when you learned something of great importance, perhaps even the very first time you learn what it was like to learn. You could have been with a group of people or with someone older and when that pleasant memory comes to mind move your right index finger. (wait) Good! It is times like that when we learn... when everything seems right, if sounds good and it feels real, that it's **like this voice**... that is guiding us. A voice of support, a voice of wisdom, a voice of encouragement. I have a voice like that.... and when you listen for what you **want to learn** you can **hear this voice**. This is your voice. And if you listen... if you truly listen you can **hear this voice** this voice speaking to you right from the center of who you are. Listen.... listen ... and when you **hear this voice** ... move your right index finger. (wait) Good! This is your voice and you can always rely on it ... to give you what you **want to know** ... that will help you... that will guide you ... **that feels good**.*

Listen. Listen... *and just let this voice repeat and repeat ... right now ... out loud ... to yourself... inside... all that you want to know ...**thats good**... about yourself.*

(End of induction)

Mind Control Hypnosis

You have a very strong mind and you **like learning about yourself**... to **find new ways** that will allow you to **make changes** ... **that you want** which will feel good for you... and it doesn't even matter if you know exactly what those changes are ... it's only important that you **learn and enjoy** as this process naturally takes place... at the deepest level... you realize that there is a part of you that can make changes... wonderful powerful changes... in any area of your life ...because you have throughout your life always made changes ... even now... you're not the same person you were a year ago... or ten years ago... because you've learned ... many things since then... and you realize that there is much more for you that is possible.

Even as you imagine how you wish to **feel more fulfilled** with who you are as you **see yourself at a future time** clearly in your mind... you've already made those changes... being more open to learn... **you have a strong mind**.. and **your mind** is now ready to listen to this voice... your voice... reminding you of all the wonderful things you're learning... **that feels good.**

You understand that to make any change you can... **make that change happen**... just like you wanted... and you can also... **allow that change to happen**... naturally, easily...as if it were the simplest thing in the world to do... all you have to do is **be open**... to that change... and **put aside your doubts**... **put aside your hesitations**... and **give yourself permission** ... that will naturally allow you to **feel good about this process**... and all the other wonderful work you are doing right here, right now... at the deepest

Mind Control Hypnosis

*level of your mind... even though you don't know it ... there is a part of you that is helping you... because you are right here, right now listen to this voice... your voice... telling you just what you need... **that you want** ... it reassures you to ... **just relax** and let it happen. You don't even have to try. All you need to do is listen and let the kind words echo again and again inside **your mind** ... and you can naturally... **find resources...** that you didn't even know you had...because they are there... just waiting... waiting ... to **help yourself go deeper** into that pleasant state where this voice is now natural for you to ... **just follow along**... so that during your day... whether you're alone or with people ... on the phone ... or working here... in this way... or even in the quiet moments ... all you have to do is listen... and this voice reminds you... **you're doing fine... relax... just let it happen**...**go deeper**... **forget... trust...** your inner mind to do it's perfect work... and reassures you with all the kind words ... That you're hearing... every time you ... **just listen ...** as each word passes over you like a gentle breeze coming from that place inside where you keep everything that you know is true... and during your day... anytime... when you want to... **feel this well**... all you need to do is ... **close your eyes... and remember** ... the sound of each reassuring word... **that's always there**... giving you the encouragement you want and need.*

*You give yourself full permission to **feel good** for no reason. So just take some time to recognize the pleasant feelings that you've felt...at any time in your life... **Now**... these feeling are there... as a way to remind you... **you are***

okay... and everyday you are doing the best you can ...sometimes under demanding circumstances... That is the definition of a hero... You are a good person... you have a strong mind... that can tell the difference between this voice and the the other things you've heard yourself say.

It's true that at times we tell ourselves other things ... that are nothing more than what other people have told us about who they think we are... or who they want us to be... or what you say to yourself when you're frustrated... you can always tell what these voices are because they don't fully reassure us... in just the way that we want... so you can always recognize them at times that you're feeling bad and down on yourself... and just let them fade away... these voices don't really matter... you don't even have to think about them... their not even important... as you turn your attention to your own voice.. this voice... that completely reassures you... in all the ways... that you want.

Take a moment now you create at some level of mind... a mechanism... an endless loop of wonderful feelings, suggestions and encouragement that you're hearing by this very positive and supportive internal voice...that reminds you you are loved and supported by everything around you... knowing that all you have to do is **be**... exactly who you are... and that you are not your thoughts... thoughts are just what you tell yourself ... you are not your feelings... you are something greater... you are at the deepest level something wonderful ... and all of this is true simply because you were born ... a child ... to human parents... no matter where you go... no matter what happens around you ... there is a part of you that always knows you are a loved and perfect so that when you want to learn more about yourself and make a change... you can learn easily and with pleasure and that change can happen just the way you want... and every part of you can **make this change easy**... go ahead ... **go deeper**... and enjoy the process ...that's taking place right here... right now... as this voice... your voice ... just flows and gives all the kind words you need to **remember you're okay**... and you can feel a strength and loving energy at any time of the world around you loves you and supports you... and you don't have to do a thing... just permit it... allow it all to take place... just as you wanted.. just as you needed ...when you first came to hear this voice. ...

You see yourself standing tall, relaxed, feeling at ease and able... to accomplish each of the goals you set out to accomplish... naturally, easily as if it were the simplest thing in the world to do... you don't even have to give it a second thought.

You hear within your own mind the power of a strong internal voice...**that's always there**... putting you at ease.. and you **feel it's encouragement** ... as each word and sound support as you... to do what you need to do... this is your voice... There is always something wonderful about being who you are. Within each sound... **that you're hearing**... now and as you listen to your inner voice... there is a comfort... **that you enjoy**... learning more and more about yourself... by just following along ... and you can **welcome that comfort** ... in... deeper and deeper... so no matter where you are... you can **feel at ease**... and know that you have all the resources you need to accomplish what you want... you focus in on your what is important and you act on it naturally and easily just as you wanted to... **Go Deeper**... forget... trust your inner mind to do it's perfect work.

So that even in your dreams this voice.. your voice... can be there as a gentle guide so perhaps tonight and tomorrow too... you can begin to create a dream that will be coming together to create new possibilities... of how good you can feel about yourself ... just by learning more about who you are... and your willingness to find out more...

You give yourself full permission to **feel good** for no reason. So just take some time to recognize the pleasant feelings that you've felt...at any time in your life... **Now**... these feeling are there... as a way to remind you... **you are okay**... And you don't even have to think... about it... you don't even have to remember that... **it's there**... repeating in the back of your mind... like a constant pleasant reminder that... **you're okay** ... no matter what... It just makes you able to **feel good** that at anytime all you have to do is **just listen**...at the deepest level... It's reminding you **you're a good person**... **that feels good**... no matter where you are... it's like someone you can trust is ready to give you support and encouragement... and this person is always with you... you can enjoy anything fully... at any time... and you enjoy learning about yourself... and how you can change to suit whatever is happening ... whether alone or with people, on the phone, or just relaxing ... **like what you're doing right now.**

So all you have to do is just relax... **go deeper**... beyond any thought or memory

Mind Control Hypnosis

*because you don't have to even think... about it... create an opening and welcome in this pleasant voice... and wrap yourself around it... tighter than you've ever wrapped yourself around anything before you realize it... it creates a gentle current of pleasure **that goes deeper**... and deeper ... inside you... there is a feeling that something wonderful is about to happen... as this comfort and pleasure builds and the words wash over you like a gentle breeze... **Something wonderful is about to happen** ... and you can **now** move through the world with a sense of calm anticipation... not knowing exactly what wonderful thing you'll soon discover about yourself... and how you can enjoy things more, and more.. and more... intensely... letting this voice continue ... to encourage you to do what you want most to do... **you have the strength**... and all the resources you are just waiting for you to call upon them... NOW.*

*And even though this only took a brief minute of time you'll be amazed and surprised at how well you've done. But time doesn't even matter because of how you **feel so good** about this new feeling of control **that you feel**.*

*As you gently bring your awareness back begin to become aware that even in the silence that is around you... you can still **feel wonderful**... that this voice is there with you.*

*And if you're listening to this just prior to sleep you can easily turn off the recording and drift into a deep and restful dream ... filled **sleep.** At any other time you can find you energy returning* fully aware awake and feeling wonderful. On the count of three allow your eyes to open as bring yourself fully back and aware of the environment around you.

One... You give yourself full permission to **feel good** for no reason. So just take some time to recognize the pleasant feelings that you've felt...at any time in your life... **Now**... these feeling are there... as a way to remind you... **you are okay**...this voice will always be there as you begin to return more and more aware of my voice, the comfort of your body. Bring the energy of awareness more fully back.

Two... everything is in it's proper place as you become more and more aware awake, alert and feeling wonderful.

Three ... Take a deep breath **now! Inhale deeply**... Let your arms stretch. Let your eyes open... refreshed alert WIDE AWAKE... feeling great. OPEN YOUR EYES.

Mind Control Hypnosis

"The Importance of the Process State"

This hypnosis script is designed to demonstrate the usefulness of the hypnotic state. For the sake of jargon the "process state" is the hypnotic state and is given a different name so to present it as something unique and interesting in the subjects mind.

This script lays a foundation for everything that follows. It's objectives are as follows.

• Have the subject understand the concept of "mind control," which is to gain more flexibility in thought and behavior.

• Create a "process state" that the subject will look forward to. Within this state changes can be made.

• Have the subject gain the ability to create an internal sense of comfort and pleasure.

• Frame the words "deep" and "deeper" to mean "more comfort and more pleasure."

• To test the subject's ability to create amnesia, further demonstrating control that they have over their thoughts.

• Create an experience that is pleasant for the subject and that offers feeling of anticipation for other processes.

• Responsiveness, the ability to respond

Mind Control Hypnosis

comfortably and automatically to questions and suggestions, is established as a key to pleasure and enjoyment.

"This will only take an instant of your time to experience. The purpose of this process is to gain a clear and full understanding of how the mind works... sometime it works for us... and sometimes it works against us.. and understanding the workings of the mind you can gain control of mental processes so that life can be more enjoyable, you can **have more pleasure** and **feel completely free** from hurts worries and irritations that **your mind** can bring up by habit.

You'll learn this and **get a good feeling** for it through creating a state of learning that is called the process state that's comfortable, flexible, quick to learn, **that feels good** whenever you enter the process state you'll discover new things about yourself, **your mind** and how you can **create joy and pleasure** at will.

Each time you listen to this process from beginning to end you'll feel more comfort and ease, you'll return rested and energized feeling wonderful about yourself and your experience and learned about yourself.

Learning in the process state is not achieved by studying or by awareness of your external environment but by being able to **go deeply inside** to review, learn and **experience** what it is that's just waiting for you to be discover.

Within the process state comfort is important and a person can **feel comfort** first by simply being aware of your physical body and relaxing... **Get comfortable... now**... as your comfort grows more and more pleasant it's important that you understand that during each process you will hear the word "deeper" and all that word "deeper" is to mean is to **increase your comfort**... which will demonstrate to you by experience that you are gaining more and more control of your thoughts and **your mind.** So **begin now** to notice your body and take a few moments to **create comfort** for yourself. (pause) and as you hear the word "deeper" **increase that comfort** in what ever way is most natural and easy for you. (pause) Now **go deeper** (pause) and as you **experience more comfort** acknowledged that to yourself that you are gaining more control (pause) now **go deeper** again creating even more comfort so that each time through each process you experience a more pleasant and enjoyable sense of comfort **and trust** the process that is taking place even as you might begin to notice that on occasion **your mind** might wander which is perfectly natural and you can allow your mind to wander as you respond fully to each suggestion and to each suggestion you can **go deeper** (pause) **create more comfort** and enjoyment which is a natural part of the process state. Each time you **go deeper** you can consciously acknowledge the control that you are experiencing over your thoughts, your emotions, your body and **your mind**.

    An important part of the learning in the process state is that of easily being able to respond in simple and pleasant ways to each suggestion such as responding to the word "**deeper**" by **feeling very comfortable right now** or you'll notice that if a questioned is asked you **easily**

respond with movement of your head or a simple word "yes" or "no" and in so doing you are learning even greater control to **build that sense of comfort** in any situation, any time, and under any circumstance your ability to **feel comfort** is there as a resource for you rely on.

So, now **go deeper**, so that each word that you hear more easily begins to create it's own smooth and pleasant place – all your objections behind you – that feels natural and easy so that you are now learning more and more about yourself.

And because responding to suggestions is vital to learning in the process state **go deeper now** and when you feel the deeper sense of comfort easily nod your head or say "yes" (wait for response). Good! And each time you **respond fully** in such a way you **open yourself** to learn more... so now again **go deeper** and when you have, again nod your head or say "yes" (wait for response) Good! And will you continue to do so with each suggestion? (wait for response) Good! **Go deeper** knowing that each time you **respond fully** you will learn more and more about yourself, your world, **your mind** and gain greater and greater control.

And so you're ready to learn.

Within the mind there are many places and each place within your mind has an important role in learning. There is a place where you put things that you know are true. Things like the sun rises each morning or perhaps it's true that you feel a wonderful feeling towards someone very close to you. Take a moment and find or create that place where things are true and when you have it simply

Mind Control Hypnosis

respond with a nod or say yes. (pause) Good. Now **go deeper** and continue to respond pleasantly in just that manner. In this place where things are true you can begin to accept each pleasant change you are making as true and real for you. Each new wonderful thing that you learn about yourself can now become true because you place it right there where things are true. Take a moment to make all this true and when you are done nod your head or say "yes". (pause) Good. **Go deeper.**

With each new thing that you learn you will know it's true... now you can **make each suggestion true...that you like**... by simply allowing it to naturally fit, so comfortably into the place where things are true. So now, on a **deeper** level suggest to your **deeper** inner mind to **make that happen**... and once you have nod your head or say "yes" and allow yourself to **go deeper.** (pause)

Good. **Go deeper...** forget.... trust... your inner mind to do it's perfect work and make all that you experience here today real, right, and true for you. And so it is.

There is another place within **your mind** that you'll find quiet useful. A place far behind you where you put things that are no longer true for you and things that no longer really matter... things like you used to live in another town but now you don't, or that you used to ride a different vehicle but now you don't. Find or create that place inside **your mind now** and when you have nod your head or say yes (pause) Good. This is the place where things no longer matter and in this place you can put all your worries, all your hesitations, all your excuses and all the things that used to hold you back. Because it's so pleasant you can now let those things begin to slide or fall back there where you don't even have to think about them. They don't even really matter. As you **let that happen now** and notice it simply nod your head or say "yes" and then **go deeper.** (pause) Good.

And even further back in that place that no longer matters is all of your forgettings, all the names of people you've met just once...lost to time. All the phone numbers ... forgotten... filled with unimportant things piled **deep** and unknown... So that you can have even greater control of your mind take moment now and find that place of forgettings and you have it nod your head or say 'yes' and **go deeper** (pause)

So that you can learn even more about yourself I'd like to demonstrate the power you truly have over **your mind**... just for the even the briefest moment, in that place of forgetting, right now **put your name right there**, you might find it confusing but you **realize you're fine**, and when you've done that nod your head or say 'yes' and congratulate yourself on learning the power of control. (pause) Good. Now retrieve your name. Do you have it? (pause) Good. **Go deeper.**.. Forget... trust your **deeper** inner mind to do it's perfect work to follow each pleasant suggestion **that you like** to lead you to greater knowledge and understanding.

Now, I'm going to reveal to you a secret that prevents so many people from really learning how to enjoy life. The reason is that of judgment. We've all felt the pain of not being understood. We've all felt what it was like to have someone

Mind Control Hypnosis

reject us without ever considering what we're experiencing and feeling and in the same way by us judging we ourselves loose out on truly understanding what's possible...that can make all the difference. Before anyone can learn what it is they truly want to know, you have to experience it as real... to find the real joy, pleasure and excitement of life. Can you **see that as true?** *(pause).*

*Good. So while you're learning through this process put all your judgment aside...***go deeper***... forget... and allow yourself to simply let go and let each word wash over you as if it were your own thoughts guiding you to* **deeper** *understandings more about yourself.*

At the same time we all know what it's like have someone with your who truly understands your hopes, your fears, your feelings and desires. And to **share that openness** *one does that without judging, only accepting, what is true and real for you right now.*

(this you can repeat this paragraph at various times throughout the process) *and right now...you enjoy learning about yourself and this process of learning. You are strong and in control enough to easily* **let go** *and* **feel pleasure** *with each suggestion your mind understands, your body grows strong and you're eager to learn more...and let all your analyzing simply fall away to the place where you put things that no longer matter, it isn't important, it doesn't even matter, you don't even have to think...about it. Just enjoy and accept that you are unique with a* **deeper** *understanding of what is true and real and* important to you there is so much pleasure in letting go and learning in this way as you let each word that you hear becomes part of your own thoughts and repeats, repeats, right now, out loud, to yourself, inside, you have so much more strength, c o n t r o l and confidence in yourself. (this you can repeat at various times throughout the process)

It is only through your strength that you can **let go** and allow this learning to take place so easily that it seems like a faint and pleasant dream that fades naturally from your memory upon returning from the process state. Yet you know all of this is true.

And each time you think back to this process all you need to remember is the special feeling of knowing that you're learning...more and more about yourself ...and that you eagerly look forward to this listening to this process again and again because each time you do you instantly return to that pleasant **deep** learning state called the process state. It feels wonderful and all you have to do is let go, relax and **go deeper.**

Between now and the next process session you will discover more about who you are and new healthy things **that you enjoy**. You look forward to the next session with a calm readiness. Each day for you is special and a each night you will dream wonderful dreams that will be coming together for your greater joy and happiness now each suggestion naturally fits and is real for you. Each suggestion is right there in that part of you where you keep everything that is true.

As you look now to that place **that's true** you

can tell **it just feels right** to know you're learning in this way you have more energy throughout your day, free from worry and concern. You are changing just as you wanted, just as you needed when you first came to hear this voice. Because inside you there is a voice of confidence security, comfort and strength. This voice is your voice and it guides you revealing new and wonderful things about yourself. Liston ... Liston... as this voice echoes pleasantly at the deepest level of your inner mind whether you are asleep or awake or in this process state of learning as you are right now this voice is your true guide. There is a calm and comfort as it guides you. So that in the quiet moments of your thoughts the pleasant whispers of this voice comforts you and gives you strength. This is your voice and all of this is true.

So just let go. **Go deeper.** Forget... trust... the power of your inner mind and this voice to guide you so you don't even have to remember... that each suggestion is all part of your true self being revealed to you as each wonderful day unfolds before you there is a quiet eagerness to explore what more you can learn about yourself... explore how much more your life is getting better, better and better in every way. You truly are eager to listen to this process every day and find out more about yourself.

You now understand the importance of truly learning in the process state because you can truly test what is real and you know this is true because you are focused, relaxed and feeling absolutely wonderful about what is taking place right this very moment as each word simply washes over you...and you may begin to find that as you *focus in on the sound of each word and words of each sound that you don't know if it what you are hearing or your own thoughts and it doesn't even really matter.*

Tonight, perhaps tomorrow too, your deeper, inner mind can give you a dream, a very special dream that clarifies the problem indicates the source perhaps, but tells you quite clearly how to solve your concerns and problems now. And each night afterwards, until you understand it, until you decide to do it or not, that dream can return to you in one form or another.

And every day as you go about your business, your unconscious can find something, some thought, perception, awareness, a taste perhaps or a sensation, or even a color, that seems familiar and reminds you of something, reminds you of what your unconscious mind is trying to tell you, until you fully understand and use that understanding for you.

*Because you enjoy learning about yourself and this process of learning. You are strong and in control enough to easily **let go.** It is only through your strength that you can **let go** and feel pleasure with each suggestion your mind understands, your body grows strong and you're eager to learn more...and let all your analyzing simply fall away to the place where you put things that no longer matter, it isn't important, it doesn't even matter, you don't even have to think...about it. Just enjoy and accept that you are unique with a deeper understanding of yourself and what is true and real and important to you there is so much pleasure in letting go and learning in this way as you let each word that you hear become part of your own*

Mind Control Hypnosis

thoughts and repeat, repeat, like a comforting echo, right now, out loud, to yourself, inside, you have so much more strength, control and confidence in yourself. You have a very strong mind. You have a very strong will and it is by the strength of **your mind** and will that each time you listen to this process you will **go deeper** beyond any doubt and hesitation and enjoy the rest it gives you from concern and thought with the understanding that to learn in this process state is to **make real changes...that feels good.**

So as you gently and pleasantly emerge from this process state you will find each time you listen it becomes easier ... and easier. Each time you **go deeper** and each time you return rested, comfortable, confident in that you're doing the right thing to improve your life just the way you wanted, just as you needed when you first heard this voice and all you have to remember is that it felt wonderful and that you are changing in all the ways **that you want.**

So as you return from this pleasant process state you will feel rested and alert a wide smile will come to your face as if you were told a special secret about who you truly are eager to listen to this process every day.

And even though this only took a short **minute** you will be surprised and amazed at how well you've done. Yes, even though you've spent a short minute in this pleasant process state you will be amazed at how well you've done.

And this is so.

So gently you will guide your back from this pleasant state returning your awareness to this voice, your breathing, feeling wonderful, alert and rested. At the time your eyes open you will smile widely with a sense of ease remember clearly the joy and pleasure that you now feel so deeply.

(pause)

Take a deep breath and allow the movement to return slowly and comfortably to your body. Eyes open. Alert. Awake. Feeling absolutely wonderful."

Once the subject has returned from the process state you point out the importance of being able to respond quickly in this state, and then practice going in and out of this state on command. Also it is important to practice this while standing, moving, and walking. Once that is accomplished you suggest that as the subject walks closer and closer to their car they will enter this state and gain a new insight or feeling which they will remember and report to you the next time.

Mind Control Hypnosis

"The Source of Suffering – The Key to Freedom"

This script is designed to help the subject put aside the habit of conscious judgment when practicing hypnosis.

Objectives:

• To clearly explain that the cause of trouble is automatic and unconscious judgments.

• To have the subject willingly put aside judgments in order to experience enjoyable suggestions.

• Give suggestions during the process state that will be tested immediately after emerging from it.

• Give suggestions that will be carried out later in the absence of the operator during the days that follow and prior to the next session.

• To verify that the subject will out of habit automatically enter the process state when directed to.

The following are a few effective questions for testing the results of the last process: During the last process did he or she emerge with a broad smile? Prior to starting, did the subject appear eager and excited to participate in this process? Did the subject report any new insights or feelings from the last process? Did the subject report vivid dreams?

Mind Control Hypnosis

"Just **like this**... before... will take no time at all... It will take only an instant. The purpose of this process is to learn more about how the mind naturally works. Sometimes it works for us... to help us **feel comfortable** and to **ease all concerns**... and allows us to **go deeper within** to make new discoveries... sometimes it works against us ... making conclusions that we find out are wrong... and as you learn about **your mind** you learn more about yourself so that each new experience within the process state... creates joy and allows you to **go deeper...** than the time before .. **that feels comfortable...** simple and easy to learn in this the process state... and you know that each time you hear the words "**go deeper**" you will create more pleasant sense of comfort for your body and ...**your mind...**

So just let everything happen ... exactly as it wants to happen. Don't try to make anything happen...don't try to stop... anything from happening. Just allow everything to please itself and happen as it feels like it wants to, naturally and easily as if it were the simplest thing in the world to do...**go deeper**...and relax so that **your mind** can **let go completely** and experience to trust the process state so that you can learn what it is you need know about yourself and gain more control of your life.... ...now you can listen... listen for a voice **that you trust**... inside you is this voice... this voice has a calm comforting presence **that guides you** to make all the changes **that you need...**to enjoy life. This voice is your voice... always there like a friendly guide...and as you listen you can find that the words simply wash over you so smooth soft, like the warm touch of summer *breeze you can hear each word guiding you... and even in the quite moments of your thoughts are the gentle whispers of this voice reminding you "You're safe. Relax. Let go and let me guide you." In so doing you can enjoy...whatever you are experiencing right this very moment. ...and so it can seem like a gentle fading dream yet you know that you will respond fully, easily, naturally to each opportunity to learn. And so that you can learn **go deeper** and each time you hear the words **"go deeper"** you will go past all your conscious thoughts and **create more comfort** for yourself and your body and **your mind**.*

*And you will respond to every suggestion you hear and each time you respond to each suggestion you hear you will **go deeper** as if it were the most natural thing in the world to do. And each time you are ask to respond to a question you will nod your head or say "yes" and each time you do nod your head or say "yes" you will **go deeper** with more ease. Do you agree? (wait for response) Good! **Go deeper** as your pleasant reward for doing so well.*

You have already learned that you can learn anything as long as your allow yourself to experience it for yourself as true. This provides you with the greatest freedom and pleasure. The freedom to enjoy ...every moment... just as you are right now... you also have learned that the greatest obstacle to learning, truly learning, is the criticism and judgment of the conscious mind... to know the true limitation that of the judgment I'd like you to search your memory for a time when you criticized without being understood. (pause) do you remember that time? (wait for response) In that moment, as you relive it, it is as if you created a doorway of invitation that opened up ... but instead of the kindness of understanding thrust in is the harsh pain of judgment ...growing more painful and sharp...denying who you are... forcing your to feel it's hurt... and then comes the shame of being judged... pushing it's way deeper within you and burning at that precious part of you....until all you could do is escape... Do you remember? (wait for response) Yes. And so it is that you create the same pain when you judge and evaluate.

You can **let that go now** and **go deeper** and allow those hurts to fall away. **Let go of judging** so that you can truly learn. Because now **you are learning** how the only way to **enjoy every moment** ...**enjoy this moment**... is to **let go of judgment, go deeper** and learn from a new direction.

When you **do that now** you are free... free from hurt, free to experience new things in new ways. This provides you with a sense of meaning and comfort and you can feel that comfort right now, is this true? (response) Good!

Go deeper...forget... trust your deeper inner mind... to do it's perfect work and create more comfort for yourself, your body and **your mind. Go deeper.** (pause) **go deeper** (pause) **go deeper** because now you are ready to learn how to create true joy.

True joy, true pleasure only comes from acceptance of what is happening. Only then can you yield to the possibilities that are right in front of you and learn.

This can happen simply the moment that you become aware. The moment that you **realize now**

Mind Control Hypnosis

is the time *and you **focus in deeply** and as you **do that** it's like you **see a door in front you** and you allow that door to **open up** to let that curiosity enter you. That tingling smooth feeling of curiosity penetrating deep within you as an excitement to learn more and as it builds to rich colorful brilliance you discover that feeling of acceptance. Only by accepting can you truly learn. The acceptance guides you to open yourself to it knowing that all **this is right** and as the feeling of acceptance goes deeply inside of you with it's velvety soft warmth it becomes you and you can learn and understand even more about yourself and what is possible so with pleasure you can wrap yourself around this feeling of acceptance so that slowly, gently and in it's own time with each step toward acceptance, taking it in **go deeper**, it begins to build, stronger and stronger until you culminate in understanding and curious to learn more.*

*And so it is that one returns to curiosity... and you have that curiosity to know more about yourself and create more joy...**go deeper... forget...** trust your **deeper** inner mind to do it's perfect work so all you have to remember is that you enjoy the process state and each time that you listen to your process learning will occur on **deeper** level that ever before...you realize it the whole process is over in an instant and you fell wonderful.*

*And just listen to your inner voice, **this voice** that comforts and guides you. Each sound of each word gently washes over you like a warm caress of an angels wing so you don't even have to listen and remember you can remember to forget completely as you follow all the suggestions* without hesitation or doubt simply washing them away from all your conscious awareness because each word is a natural part of your thoughts and **your mind.** And all of this is true.

True joy, true pleasure only comes from acceptance of what is happening. Only then can you yield to the possibilities that are right in front of you and learn.

This can happen simply the moment that you **become aware**. The moment that you **realize now is the time** and you **focus in deeply** and as you **do that** it's like you **see a door in front you** and you allow that door to **open up** to let that curiosity enter you. That tingling smooth feeling of curiosity penetrating deep within you as an excitement to learn more and as it builds to rich colorful brilliance you discover that feeling of acceptance. Only by accepting can you truly learn. The acceptance guides you to **open yourself** to it knowing that all **this is right** and as the feeling of acceptance goes deeply inside of you with it's velvety soft warmth it becomes you and you can learn and understand even more about yourself and what is possible so, **with pleasure**, you can wrap yourself around this feeling of acceptance so that slowly, gently and in it's own time with each step toward acceptance, taking it in **go deeper**, it begins to build, stronger and stronger until you culminate in understanding and curious to learn more.

And so it is that one returns to curiosity... and you have that curiosity to know more about yourself and create more joy...**go deeper... forget...** trust your **deeper** inner mind to do it's perfect work so all you have to remember is that you enjoy the

Mind Control Hypnosis

*process state and each time that you listen to your process learning will occur on **deeper** level that ever before.*

And all of this is true... and will continue at a deep level of your mind unaware that you'll be pleasantly surprised at what you'll discover without meaning to discover it.

*With in **your mind**, there is that powerful place where you put all things you know are true. It is there that **make all this real** without thought, judgment and it feels so right, it feels so natural to learn in this way free from memory as each word slides **deeply** into that place where things are true.*

*You don't even have to remember ...**all of this is true**... you can forget to remember or remember to forget what it is that you're already allowing yourself to discover on your own ...naturally, easily, and all you have to do is let go and let this voice, your voice, guide you repeating, repeating, right now, out loud to yourself inside is that comforting voice guiding you and you can easily respond without thought or judgment because all of this is true, is it not?*

*...and just allow your head to nod or say "yes" and go deeper. (wait) and to make this natural, easy, enjoyable and fun let any conscious memory or awareness of each suggestion disappear so you that you can learn effortlessly...let it fall away into the place behind you all your forgettings because remembering doesn't even matter when you learn in this pleasant manner and each time you remember to forget you demonstrate to yourself on a deep level the control you have over **your mind**.*

To prove to your deeper inner mind the

ease of your learning upon returning form the process state you will begin to laugh uncontrollably and for no apparent reason and free from memory of this suggestion you will find yourself enjoying laughing without control just because it feels right. So as you hear these words echoing within **your mind** your deeper inner mind accept them naturally and easily free from judgment or memory ...gone... forget ... trust your deeper inner mind to carry out each suggestion because you want to learn more and more more about yourself...and upon returning form the process state you will begin to laugh uncontrollably and for no apparent reason and free from memory of this suggestion you will find yourself enjoying laughing without control just because it feels right.

    Go deeper...now ... with each time you listen this enjoyable process you will go deeper... deeper and deeper ... each time deeper than the time before... You enjoy listening every day to the process given you so that you can learn about yourself and gain more control of the world around you.

    Each day you enter deep into the process state you return rested, energized, alert and enjoying life more. Each day you enter deep into the process state you return rested, energized, alert and enjoying life more.

    And this is true...is it not? ...and just allow your head to nod or say "yes" and go deeper. (wait) Good and so it is that your deeper inner mind can now do all the work for you automatically, instantly, so that you don't have work, to try or even to think...all you have to do is let your deeper inner mind hear each word as right for

Mind Control Hypnosis

you and you will make it your own thoughts...erasing any memory of the words so that everything you want happens just as you want it and it's a wonderful surprise.

You are surprised at what you are learning and that you have never learned it before in your life is so exciting to discover these new things and new things about you. The excitement follows you each day as you look forward to the next process learning...following you just as this voice follows you because this is your voice and it feels ... just right to learn in this way.

Go deeper...forget *trust your deeper inner mind to do it's perfect work and carry out each suggestion without effort and free from thought and even though you have only spent a brief minute with the process state you realize the freedom you are gaining as you learn in this manner.* **Go deeper.**

So for now as you **go deeper** *allow a part of* **your mind** *visualize in an easy natural way the mind being rewired, reprogrammed to* **experience joy, pleasure** *at each suggestion you hear in the process state and because all of this happens without your effort or conscious awareness forget the suggestion completely and let it happen naturally, easily and automatically like it were a pleasant and reassuring habit.*

And so that you learn and enjoy and enjoy the learning Over the next few days automatically, free from thought or effort you'll notice yourself relaxing quietly and remembering this voice ... taking a whole moment to yourself... to enjoy the process state... all on your own ... and being completely safe and secure and surprised at how

Mind Control Hypnosis

deep *you go...all the way down... only doing this in times when your daily activities allow it ... without warning while in a safe environment... automatically you find yourself enjoying the process state and being so surprised you have to tell me at our next meeting.*

*Thats right....so that you learn and enjoy and enjoy the learning Over the next few days automatically, free from thought or effort or memory of these words you'll notice yourself relaxing quietly and remembering this voice ... taking a whole moment to yourself... to enjoy the process state... all on your own ... and being completely safe and secure and surprised at how **deep** you go...all the way down... only doing this in times when your daily activities allow it ... without warning while in a safe environment... automatically you find yourself enjoying the process state and being so surprised you have to tell me at our next meeting.*

And your inner mind agrees to this so that you can now nod your head or say 'yes' and this is true, is it not? (wait).

*And each time we meet you will be ready to learn more and go deeper so that your mind is ready to make changes **that will create pleasure** in every level of your life.*

*And this is true and will be true from this time forward because you are automatically placing each suggestion, each word from this voice, your voice, right there where you put everything **that is true**... and as you **listen from that place where things are true** you will always **hear this voice** guiding you to learn more and make the right changes ...whether you are learning in the process* state or fully alert, on the phone or in any setting this voice is there comforting you, supporting you... completely in every area of life.

Because you enjoy learning about yourself and this process of learning. You are strong and in control enough to easily **let go.** It is only through your strength that you can **let go** and feel pleasure with each suggestion your mind understands, your body grows strong and you're eager to learn more...and let all your analyzing simply fall away to the place where you put things that no longer matter, it isn't important, it doesn't even matter, you don't even have to think...about it. Just enjoy and accept that you are unique with a deeper understanding of yourself and what is true and real and important to you there is so much pleasure in letting go and learning in this way as you let each word that you hear become part of your own thoughts and repeat, repeat, like a comforting echo, right now, out loud, to yourself, inside, you have so much more strength, control and confidence in yourself. You have a very strong mind. You have a very strong will and it is by the strength of **your mind** and will that each time you listen to this process you will **go deeper** beyond any doubt and hesitation and enjoy the rest it gives you from concern and thought with the understanding that to learn in this process state is to **make real changes...that feels good.**

Now... inside **your mind** I'd like you create a event that I will vividly describe to you... of a time in the future... Where you can instantly enter the process state just as you are now... so that each time you are ready and **feel anticipation** for entering the process state you **go deeper** and more enjoyably than the time before you know it you are enjoying the process state... as you create this event **inside your mind** naturally easily by simply hearing the words "**go deeper**" you create an opening to allow the process state in and you embrace it tightly... and so it is with each imagining of a future time you clearly see, crisply hear and dramatically feel yourself wrapping yourself around the this wonderful and enjoyable state of mind ...and you are ready to learn.

And so she did imagine that just as she was described... is was all so clear to her... she was there at that moment hearing the words "**go deeper**" and she felt the words pull at her like strong and caring arms... all around her was nothing but this voice... her voice that echoed all her kindest thoughts so it was so easy to follow... so simple to just let go... **deeper and deeper** than the time before... and even after she remembered only wanting waiting and anticipating the next occasion that she could return... It was all so clear to her as she heard the words and felt their warm touch...

That's right you see so clearly that time in the future...any time in the future... where you hear the words "**go deeper**" and feel swiftly returning **deeper** than the time before...

So as you gently and pleasantly emerge from this process state you will find each time you listen it becomes easier ... and easier. Each time you **go deeper** and each time you return rested, comfortable, confident in that you're doing the right thing to improve your life just the way you wanted, just as you needed when you first heard this voice and all you have to remember is that it felt wonderful and that you are changing in all the ways **that you want**... and only a moment has past.

So as you return from this pleasant process state you will feel rested and alert a wide smile will come to your face as if you were told a special secret about who you truly are eager to listen to this process every day...and only a moment has past.

And even though this only took a short **minute** you will be surprised and amazed at how well you've done. Yes, even though you've spent a short **minute** in this pleasant process state you will be amazed at how well you've done.

And this is so.

So gently you will guide your back from this pleasant state returning your awareness to this voice, your breathing, feeling wonderful, alert and rested. At the time your eyes open you will smile widely with a sense of ease remember clearly the joy and pleasure that you now feel so deeply.

(pause)

Take a deep breath and allow the movement to return slowly and comfortably to your body. Eyes open. Alert. Awake. Feeling absolutely wonderful.

Once the subject has returned from the process state you point out the importance of being able to respond quickly in this state and then practice going in and out of this state on command. Also important to practice this standing and moving, walking. Once that is accomplished you suggest that as the subject walks closer and closer to their car

Mind Control Hypnosis

they will enter this state and gain a new insight or feeling which they will remember and report to you at the next process.

Mind Control Hypnosis

"The Power of the Process State"

Objectives:

• Train and test the subject to enter the process state on the command "go deeper."

• Create amnesia on command.

• Test to see if the suggestions given in previous processes were successfully carried out.

• If all tests are successful, suggest a new behavior be performed that is outside of the subject's norm. The new behavior is done with great pleasure and carried out without the subject's memory of the suggestions, but the subject will be eager to report it to you.

• Frame the unconscious mind as the place where creativity, flexibility and enjoyment come from via the process state. Get confirmation and agreement.

• Frame the conscious, thinking mind as the reason they have not experienced deep, profound and consistent joy and pleasure in their life. Get confirmation and agreement. Put aside all conscious awareness to maximize true enjoyment.

• Suggestions of vivid and pleasurable dreams that will eagerly be reported at the next process.

A few questions which can test the effectiveness of the last process are did the subject report on automatically entering the process state and not need to be prompted to tell you? Did the subject laugh spontaneously upon emerging from the last process? Did the subject report a new insight as they walked to their car after the last process?

*"**Go deeper.** The purpose of this process is you to learn more about who you are and to explore further .. your response-ability ... to open you up... for beyond question or doubt ... and inside **your mind** you will ... have all the resources.. you need to ... just let go... give yourself permission to ... live freely... from the burdens and conditions of the world... let go ... let completely go... and **go deeper**... **inside your mind**... so that ... you will ... learn to **get the benefits you desire** ... as you let go completely... trusting... that you're in the right place .. at the right time... to give yourself permission to enjoy what is happening ... right this very moment ... free from doubt or hesitation ...*

*Now **go deeper** and allow your powerful inner mind to demonstrate to you it's true power that only the inner mind can reveal to you... with this process state you will learn to enjoy more choices and more options because you know that the more choices you have the more free you are in every situation ... and begin to let the old conscious mind full of thoughts and worries just slip away... and drift off... freeing you... completely to all the way inside ...perhaps you feel as if you're floating or if you're gently falling or perhaps you will no longer be aware of the you that is experiencing this pleasure... and it really doesn't even matter because you know it's right and good*

Mind Control Hypnosis

... and you can begin to listen to this voice ... your voice ...that gently guides you...

So that you can learn exactly how to be free, truly free, hear this voice, your voice say the words **go deeper** and allow it all to just happen, naturally easily as if it were the simplest thing in the world to because you have permitted it.

Go beyond any doubt or hesitation go beyond the awareness of the body... **go deeper** to the place of dreams... these can be dreams of sleep or dreams of possibilities but however it is you naturally **have these dreams** you will be the dream **you are dreaming** so that it doesn't even seem real it only seems so pleasant that you just want it to happen ... allow it to happen ... permit it to happen just as it does happen ... so that you experience the dream so easily just as I describe it focus yourself on each word completely... so you hear only the sound of each word and the word of each sound that each word you are hearing is your own thought ... and it's so nice not to worry about what to think or what others think ...it's nice to just go so deeply that all you are is a dream of pleasure and with each suggestion you hear you respond within this dream ... that's right with each word you hear of each suggestion you hear you respond and each time you respond you enjoy... deeply enjoy responding ... just as you hear ... free...completely free from hesitation as if it were the most natural thing in the world to do...

Now... so that you learn and enjoy this process of responding to each learning I'd like to demonstrate to you the true power of your inner mind I'd like you to remember the part of the mind where you put all things that are true... the place where you know the sun appears each day is true... the part of the mind where you keep the knowledge of those people whom you care about is true... and when you have that place in your mind... in a calm firm voice say "Yes". (wait) Good... very good now **go deeper** ... and when you want to make a change a part of you and a true part of you life all you have to do is place it there where you put all things you know are true... and even as you remember the wonderful changes that you've made you now can see them there where you all things that are true... isn't this so? (wait) and you can continue to respond in just that manner and go deeper each time... will you not? (wait) Good. Go deeper.

And you can now remember how you learned about the part of your mind where you put things that don't even really matter... it's also the part of you where you put things that just used to be true for you but aren't any more... for example it used to be true that you lived in another place but now you don't and that is now in that part where things used to be true... can you see that now? (wait) Good.

Now even further back behind you in the place where you put things that don't even really matter is the place of all your forgettings ... all the phone number that are lost to time... all the names of those faint people you've met just once... forgotten... this is the place of your forgettings ... and so that you can learn even more let me know when you've found that place of forgettings by saying and a calm firm voice "yes" (wait).

Good!

Now to demonstrate the true power of your

deeper inner mind... In the place where you put all your forgettings just **place your name right there** ... and once you have **go deeper** and tell me that you have done that in a calm firm voice say "yes". (wait) Good!

That's right for now you can just let it go... just let the name go completely... and **feel just fine**.... is it gone? (wait) Good! And permit it to remain there comfortably for now ... and to further demonstrate the power within your inner mind allow your eyes to open comfortably while still in the process state.. (wait) ... good ... and you have forgotten something haven't you? (yes) Did you **forget the name** completely? (yes)... and you feel very comfortable don't you in this state? (yes) You're doing very well and learning the real power of your inner mind and the power of the process state... **go deeper**... forget... trust your inner mind to do it's perfect work...without doubt or hesitation and follow each suggestion so that you can learn and as you learn you respond just you're ask to respond.

And so that you can learn powerfully within this state I'm going to ask you to let everything go just like you did the name ... let everything simple fall far far far behind you in the place of all forgettings... and you will respond to me as I ask by saying yes. Will you do that now? (yes).

Now I want to reveal to you the secret of how you have suffered for so long ... your suffering is because you have used your conscious mind to think and evaluate and to judge... it is this conscious mind that has caused all your pain and caused all the pain of the world... and as you are now experiencing the power of the **deeper** inner mind

Mind Control Hypnosis

you see the inner mind is there to help you enjoy whatever it is you are feeling, enjoy whatever your experiencing right this very moment... You inner mind has all the secrets that you have been looking for and now you are ready to learn.

You can now imagine with your mind and see with your eyes a cord of light that comes from you to me... feel the warmth of that cord of light and it pulsates the connection that is between us ... do you feel it now? (wait) ....let that connection grow stronger... brighter ... now warmer... and feel the wonderful emotion that you are feeling from me now... do you feel it? (wait) does it feel wonderful? (wait)

Each time you hear a suggestion in the process state you create an opening ... create an opening of **connection** between us ... and you allow this warm flowing connection to enter inside... **your mind**... and grow stronger... allowing it to build...building more and more... stronger and stronger until is fills throughout who you are and reveals to you a wonderful excitement... which allows you to **go deeper now**... revealing an excitement ... about what you can do ... notice the tingling of this excitement as you... **let it in** ... let go further inside ...humming and vibrating... as the excitement builds... getting stronger... and rushes through every part of you with an explosion that show you a powerful sense of ...certainty ... yes certainty that what you are doing is right...certainty that each soft word you hear can repeat firmly within **your mind**... so that certainty becomes firmer, stronger, and you feel the power of this firm and ridged, as it builds and explodes with an absolute ...**conviction** ...to repeat

Mind Control Hypnosis

the process so that you can **enjoy the all that you are learning** ... conviction...smooth and velvety... **like the comfort you feel right now** ... that touches you at the deepest part of who you are... as that conviction builds and culminates naturally as if all on it's own ... it reveals a **joy** ... a joy to be learning so powerfully ... in this way... and in this way it will happen
...again and again... each time in the process state... naturally, easily... just as you've always wanted and enjoy to learn in this manner.

Good! And all of this has happened because you've followed my suggestions so perfectly isn't that true? And you want to follow my suggestions. Is this true? (wait) and you will follow each suggestion I give you completely because you enjoy the process state and you know that it pleases me and you want the success and that you are very pleased by the success that you have received...and that pleases you very much does it not? (wait) and it pleases me to see that are succeeding and achieving what you want... and you enjoy pleasing me in this way...and you enjoy pleasing me...by successfully following each of my suggestions... Do you ...**agree with me**? And you want to please me don't you? (wait) Yes, as you please me your success will grow.. and you have many successes by simply doing what I have asked you to do...

...in your mind review all the wonderful success and joy that you have been able to achieve...like being able to sleep like a baby at night and awakening fully refreshed and have so much more energy in your life... for you to ...accomplish ... more ...of the things that you want to accomplish.. and you've done this all by learning in the process state and the power of my voice... so in order to gain even more control over your life... even more control over your emotions... I want you... to focus on the feeling of conviction... of making a decisions and knowing beyond doubt of hesitation that you will carry it out with all your force, will and being... when you feel that sense of conviction now say "yes" and feel it being said with that conviction...

Good and say yes again increasing that conviction.. and realize that any time you respond to me by answering "yes" or by nodding your head you will do so feeling that sense of conviction and you realize how... **this will benefit you**...will you agree...this is true?(yes)

Excellent! You are doing very well and now continue to build that sense of conviction ...when ever you respond to me do you... agree with me completely?

Now you have learned to feel a sense of conviction, it will benefit you to bring about other powerful and positive emotions... so focus now on gratitude...focus on the things that you ...**feel very grateful** for... NOW... those things that support you...and help you.. those blessings in your life...now.... the gratitude for being able to... **follow every suggestion** so well you've learned so perfectly... following without question or doubt ... being so grateful... to have that wonderful experience of having me in your life... as a friend and trainer... do you **feel that gratitude now with conviction**?
(wait)

Wonderful! You are doing Very well ...you are

doing very well indeed...and I appreciate your eagerness to ... **follow every suggestion I give you**... you have a very strong mind...and a very powerful will.. and now, in order for you to gain even more control of your mind and life.... think of those things that you know are true.. **that's good**... because you are going to focus on a sense of certainty.... **CERTAINTY**... the knowledge of what you realize is true... the certainty that the process state is pleasant and enjoyable ...and the certainty that you have the ability to learn and improve simply because you **follow every suggestion I give you**.. without question or doubt... and the certainty that comes from your ability to **enjoy doing that**.. in the process state...NOW.. do you now **feel that certainty** with that sense of conviction and gratitude? (wait)

Now, In order for you to even further improve your life and your flexibility in how you respond to the world ... I want you ...to **focus on JOY**... joy... of just being alive and being able to make changes.. **that you want**.. and the joy of living life fully... the joy of being in my presence ....and the joy of knowing that you are safe and secure ...and can **trust me**....fully and completely... focus on that joy.. now...and all the joys of your life..and when you feel that joy with conviction, gratitude and certainty...say "yes"(wait).

Yes it is true. You do feel the joy of simply giving yourself to me and my voice...don't you? (wait) Following each suggestions is your pleasure and you can now gain even more joy, gratitude and pleasure by focusing on the other ways and feelings that you are now even more capable of expressing...

There are many pleasures in life... emotional and physical pleasures.. there is the pleasure that is so... indulgent ...that you must have it... you want it ...it is that power pleasure of sexual pleasure...the wonderful powerful pleasure of sexual orgasm... and now on let that pleasure of orgasm build as you say "Yes" to accept each suggestion. (wait)

That is right.... **you mind** is very powerful and you enjoy following my suggestions and commands. This is true isn't it? (wait)

And you want to follow my suggestions and my commands. Is this true? And you will follow and obey each suggestion and command because you know that it pleases me and that you will learn more... and you are very pleased with your success...are you not? (wait) and it pleases me to see that you are succeeding and achieving what you want... and you enjoy pleasing me in this way... you enjoy pleasing me... by successfully following each of my suggestions.... Do you... agree with me? (wait) And you want to please me don't you? Yes, and as you please your success will grow... and the more you please me the more success you will experience... this as the greatest learnings of your life... this learning is that all your life it has been your conscious mind that held you back from learn... your conscious mind has held you back from having real joy and pleasure... your conscious mind has been your true enemy... preventing you from having what you want and making all the problems you've experienced.... but in the process state you have gone past every part of the conscious mind to really learn...from me

Mind Control Hypnosis

and your inner mind... your inner mind has shown you the true freedom of and joys that you are capable of and still you realize that you no longer remember your name and it feels okay doesn't it? (wait)... in fact there is no longer is a YOU there that is holding you back...from learning and enjoying life...and from this time forward you go into the process state you will go so deeply that you will easily follow each suggestion instantly carrying them out without doubt or hesitation and then erasing them from your memory... It will have only been an instant past of powerful learning and you'll have a wonderful feeling and smile on your face...as you deeper inner mind erases all memory ...like erasing a magnetic tape... or wiping away chalk from a chalk board...gone... it no longer even matters... and you will continue to carry out each suggestion instantly and easily and then erase the memory from your mind...like erasing a magnetic tape... letting it go... it doesn't' even matter, it's no longer important.... [new behavior] and automatically you are producing a wonderful new behavior... a behavior that helps ... that's new... throughout the course of your day ... each time you pass by a mirror... or each time you see your reflection in a surface a mere second will pass in your mind... and you will here a voice... this voice... your voice... and you will smile ... a smile that you know a very special secret ... a secret that is held deep within you... and a warmth will build in you as you continue with your activities... this will only be an instant of time... throughout the course of your day ... each time you pass by a mirror... or each time you see your reflection in a surface a mere second will pass in your mind... and you will here a voice... this voice... your voice... and you will smile ... a smile that you know a very special secret ... a secret that is held deep within you... and a warmth will build in you as you continue with your activities... this will only be an instant of time... throughout the course of your day ... each time you pass by a mirror... or each time you see your reflection in a surface a mere second will pass in your mind... and you will here a voice... this voice... your voice... and you will smile ... a smile that you know a very special secret ... a secret that is held deep within you... and a warmth will build in you as you continue with your activities... this will only take an instant of time...

Now go deeper.

[vivid and pleasant dreams]
    and now I speak only to your deeper inner mind... between now and the next process we do together ...the deeper inner mind will create for you dreams... as you sleep so soundly at night... and instantly **fall**... into the state of deep restful sleep... as you rest... vivid and pleasant dreams will arise ... vivid dreams that will be coming together... to show the powerful changes...that are taking place as the each moment passes... and as they reveal themselves to you ...you will feel desire to share them with me ... because your inner mind hears the suggestions and responds ... your inner minds knows the desire to make changes... **that helps you**... **that's right** ... you'll know the dreams to describe to me without knowing why...because each suggestion is there and you respond so naturally to learning in this

Mind Control Hypnosis

manner....between now and the next process we do together ...the deeper inner mind will create for you dreams... as you sleep so soundly at night... and instantly **fall**... into the state of deep restful sleep... as you rest... vivid and pleasant dreams will arise ... vivid dreams that will be coming together... to show the powerful changes...that are taking place as the each moment passes... and as they reveal themselves you will feel desire to share them with me ... because your inner mind hears the suggestions and responds ... your inner minds knows the desire to make changes... **that helps you**... **that's right** ... you'll know the dreams to describe to me without knowing why...because each suggestion is there and you respond so naturally to learning in this manner....

    Now... inside **your mind** I'd like you create a event that I will vividly describe to you... of a time in the future... Where you can instantly enter the process state just as you are now... so that each time you are ready and **feel anticipation** for entering the process state you **go deeper** and more enjoyably than the time before you know it you are enjoying the process state... as you create this event **inside your mind** naturally easily by simply hearing the words *"***go deeper***"* you create an opening to allow the process state in and you embrace it tightly... and so it is with each imagining of a future time you clearly see, crisply hear and dramatically feel yourself wrapping yourself around the this wonderful and enjoyable state of mind ...and you are ready to learn.

    And so she **did** imagine that just as she was described... it was all so clear to her... she was there at that moment hearing the words *"***go deeper***"* and she felt the words pull at her like strong and caring arms... all around her was nothing but this voice... her voice that echoed all her kindest thoughts so it was so easy to follow... so simple to just let go... **deeper and deeper** than the time before... and even after she remembered only wanting... waiting and anticipating the next occasion that she could return... It was all so clear to her as she hear the words and felt their warm touch...

That's right you see so clearly that time in the future...any time in the future... where you hear the words **"go deeper"** and feel swiftly returning **deeper** than the time before...

[return name & identity]

Now you can recover your name from that place of forgettings ... Now as you return from this process state you know exactly who you are... you have your name... you have your name because now it will serve you...

So as you gently and pleasantly emerge from this process state you will find each time you listen it becomes easier ... and easier. Each time you **go deeper** and each time you return rested, comfortable, confident in that you're doing the right thing to improve your life just the way you wanted, just as you needed when you first heard this voice and all you have to remember is that it felt wonderful and that you are changing in all the ways **that you want.**

So as you return from this pleasant process state you will feel rested and alert a wide smile will come to your face as if you were told a special secret about who you truly are eager to listen to this process every day.

And even though this only took a short **minute** you will be surprised and amazed at how well you've done. Yes, even though you've spent a short minute in this pleasant process state you will be amazed at how well you've done.

And this is so.

So gently you will guide your back from this pleasant state returning your awareness to this voice, your breathing, feeling wonderful, alert and rested. At the time your eyes open you will smile widely with a sense of ease remember clearly the joy and pleasure that you now feel so deeply. (pause.)"

"Take a deep breath and allow the movement to return slowly and comfortably to your body. Eyes open. Alert. Awake. Feeling absolutely wonderful."

Once the subject has returned from the process state you point out the importance of being able to respond quickly in this state and then practice going in and out of this state on command. Also, it is important to practice this standing and moving, walking. Once that is accomplished, in the process state, you suggest that as they are just about to leave the building they will remember that they have forgotten something and return to find it. When they return they will realize they have everything they need with them and have no memory of this suggestion.

Mind Control Hypnosis

"Restraint as Liberation"

Objectives:

• Confirm that all process suggestions were carried out. If not, the previous process is repeated. Emphasis is given on how much more joy, pleasure, and understanding will be available when each suggestion is carried out effortlessly.

• Re-frame for the subject that true power lies in the ability to restrain oneself, and give an experience of that degree of control using bondage.

• Create a process-oriented identity and name for how the subject would ideally respond in every situation with these new learnings.

'Are you ready? Good... **go deeper***.*

The purpose of this process is so that you can learn even more on new level, a **deeper** *level about what you are capable of ...so much more than you ever thought possible ...as someone who deeply values the process state I'd like you to notice where you are at ...and ...* **go deeper...deeper now** *than you've ever been... going past all your thoughts and judgments that have held you back ...knowing that each time you hear the words* **"go deeper"** *you can just... let go.. . Let go completely and allow yourself the real freedom to learn about yourself...learn about how you can* **just relax** *... relax away time, relax away space, relax away awareness... of all your limitations. Just* **go deeper** *and enjoy fully and*

Mind Control Hypnosis

completely what it is you were meant to do, what you were meant to truly feel... a wonderful sense of comfort and pleasure can begin as you open yourself to new learnings and experiences **that means so much to you...** and as the body you inhabit just now relaxes away **your mind** can just listen to each word... the sound of each word and words of each sound ...that doesn't even matter to your conscious mind as your deeper inner mind hears each word with complete understanding and agreement it just feels like the sounds of each word are warmly moving through you as you hear them in just the same way you hear your own thoughts... and every time you you hear the words in my voice say **"go deeper"** instantly you go further and further than the time before. So just let go and let that comfort begin to build stronger and stronger as you open yourself to it and let it in so that the voice you hear, this voice, your voice can be received just wrap yourself around the words, wrap yourself around the voice and bring the soft smooth sound **deeper and deeper** so that it feels just right, it feels like it's a part of you and you wrap yourself around it tighter and tighter ... wrap yourself around it tighter than you've ever wrap yourself around anything before and ... **go deeper inside your mind** beyond even thought...so that all there is is this timeless moment ...that only seems like an instant... and time didn't pass at all for her...and as she looked at me there was something she could see about me... she just saw some part of my face **that fascinated her** as i read she couldn't move or look past it ... felt so comfortable to just fall into that voice and how it to become the only thing in her awareness. .. and in that moment she began to feel that it was all right... that what *made sense was to go past judging and thinking and let it all happen just the way it was supposed to happen...just the way it was meant to happen .... and she could take her eyes away... the voice she heard was her voice speaking her thoughts and feelings... so she just followed along naturally, easily and everything she needed to do she knew was right...there in that part where things are true...for you there is always a part that knows you can listen and follow along ... a part that is ten times stronger than even you are... that enjoys this process... and will follow each suggestion naturally as if it were so easy... this part that is ten times stronger than even you are will hear every word... and respond ...by simply answering 'yes' or doing what is asked ... in the process state... whether standing or sitting or awake or in the process state... on the phone ... or with friends ... this wonderful part will **find pleasure** in carrying out each suggestion and will **answer yes**...when asked... Is this true? (wait)*

[Amnesia for name and feel great about it]
*[foreshadow that by end of this process **if** you do well you can create a New Name that reps you in process state that will enhance your learning– give this suggestion 3 times]*

*Good! Now **Go deeper** and find that place within your mind where you forget... where you put things that no longer matter... there far behind you where go all the things that are lost to time...unimportant... forgotten... they don't even matter... and so that you can learn even more about yourself ... when you have that place of* forgettings say "yes" (wait). Good! Now you have a very strong mind so with the strength inside **your mind**... in that place of forgetting place your name right there...and **feel wonderful...Place your name right there and feel wonderful**... when you've done that say 'yes' (wait) good...and you'll notice that no matter how hard you look you can't find it and you feel wonderfully free from that label that others have given you... don't you? (wait). So just enjoy that freedom enjoy it completely... create an opening that will let that freedom inside and free you more and more...until it explodes with understanding that you've have now a chance... if you do well... to create your own name... That's right if you do well ... before you return from this pleasant process state you'll have a chance to choose your own name... your new name that will help you learn even more... that understanding has a strength a firmness that grows inside of you... wanting to do well ... and pleasing me so that you may choose your new name... and you would like that don't you? (wait).

That's correct, you had no choice in the past so you had to live up to the name people gave you... but now it's gone and you are free... to feel. to enjoy what you enjoy doing right now... and you enjoy following these suggestions and pleasing me and feeling this wonderful, don't you? (wait) Good... and if you do well and please me you will choose a new name for the you that you want to be... responding naturally and easily so you can learn more and more about the power you feel right now...

In the past a lot of things were true and you now know you can go past the past and create what you truly want and enjoy... in the past you had no choice so you had to live up to the name people gave you... but now it's gone and you are free... to feel... to enjoy what you enjoy doing right now... and you enjoy following these suggestions and pleasing me and feeling this wonderful... and if you do well and please me you will choose a new name for the you that you want to be... responding naturally and easily so you can learn more and more about the power you feel right now... **so go deeper**... go even **deeper**

[Yes set with Mag Grid – yes -> certainty -> conviction -> pleasure -> orgasm. then ask "do you want to learn more about how to enjoy life?"]

...allow your self to respond completely to what you are learning to enjoy ... to my suggestions ...so that as you experience this pleasant state you can respond completely to my questions with a yes or no and each time go deeper... do you understand? (wait) Good.. so **go deeper** just as you will each time to you **respond this way to me**... now ....I want you... I deeply want you... to bring up the feeling of certainty... the certainty that you are learning and enjoying this process... bring up the feeling of certainty... and when you feel that certainty, with all your feelings say "yes" (wait)... and **go deeper...** now with that certainty bring forth the feeling of conviction... that what you are doing is right... bring up the that feeling of conviction and add it to your certainty and when you feel is ...with all your heart... say "yes" (wait) Good... now combine that with pleasure ... pleasure of knowing you are learning about control and freedom... powerful joyous pleasure and add that to your certainty and conviction and when you **feel that pleasure** say "yes"...Good. And you enjoy this don't you? (wait)... and enjoy responding so powerfully to each suggestion... don't you" (wait).

There are many pleasures in life... emotional and physical pleasures.. there is the pleasure that is so... indulgent ...that you must have it... you want it ...it is that power pleasure of sexual pleasure...the wonderful powerful pleasure of sexual orgasm... and now on let that pleasure of orgasm build as you say "Yes" to accept each suggestion. (wait)

That is right.... **your mind** is very powerful and you enjoy following my suggestions and commands. This is true isn't it? (wait)

Good! Now **go deeper**... forget... trust your inner mind to do it's perfect work and follow each suggestion you hear from the sound of my voice ...as you let each sound of each word create an opening and you let it in....wrap yourself around each word ...each sound of my voice... so that each word creates a color or truth... a warm touch... a powerful acceptance of what you know is true for you.

[reframe restraint as power]

... and there was a woman who had left who she **thought** she was behind ... to learn more about what she could be... even more that could be imagined... and she realized that there was so much pain that she had felt... because she was trapped by what she only thought was real... she protected herself by holding back on exploring what was

*possible and she lost out ... lost out completely... because when she held herself back ... she didn't mean to... she **closed off** all possibilities of learning...You've always had to hold yourself back... and because you didn't understand what you now know... you did it so as not be judged or criticized... now you understand even more... that it is you who have control of how you evaluate what you experience ...this as meaningful...and you are now able to enjoy so much more than you ever thought possible...isn't this true? (wait) Now, because your mind is under a greater control you can change your holding back into a strength... because now, in your restraint, you are free to experience anything ...**that you decide**... don't you? (wait) So now you can surrender yourself completely and anticipate the joy and pleasure **that you will create**. For it is in complete restraint that you can see new directions of possibilities. Don't you? (wait)*
[subject creates catalepsy and within that restraint creates pleasure that is moved through the body]

*So to learn this **I want you**... to still your body completely... telling each muscle in the body to re- main still... unmoving ...so that all that your body can do is answer me... and when you've done that say 'yes' (wait) Good. Now by doing that begin to create a feeling of joy and pleasure **that you can feel** ...within the right hand... feel the warmth, the color, the texture of that delicious pleasure within your right hand... and when you have that .. say 'yes' (wait) ... good! Now move all of that pleasure to your left hand ... feeling it, tasting and drinking it the color of pleasure **that***

you feel in the left hand... and when you have that pleasure... say 'yes' (wait). Now your mind is under even greater control and you can move that pleasure to where ever I want... so gently move that pleasure to your right shoulder ... and when you have say 'yes'.

(Proceed with moving the pleasure throughout various points in the body always always having the subject confirm with "yes").

...and all of this is done within your **new** understanding of restraint... and this is pleasurable isn't it?

So take this knowledge with you and as you do... allow your eyes to fully see the power that your mind is under (suggest her eyes open and see to it that she is looking at you while still in the process state). Do you see the power your mind is under? (wait) Do you feel pleasure at this power? Feel this power as a massive mountain... it fills your vision... it reaches farther than you can extend... wherever you reach you can feel it... and the bigger you discover and accept and know that it is-- the more powerful it is-- the more this limitless power protects you... and the safer that you feel... the more powerful it is, the more you surrender to it, because the bigger and more powerful you admit that it is, the smaller and safer you are, and the more it protects you.

...and all of this is done within your **new** understanding of restraint... and this is pleasurable isn't it? (wait) Do you agree to let your restraint be your strength (Holding up cuff/restraints).

(put the subject through a series of restraint drills and following directions while in restraints confirming that she finds pleasure in each activity.)

Mind Control Hypnosis

[restraint drills showing pleasure about consent -> agreement to enjoy pleasing the operator]

(remove restraints) ...and now I'm going to ask you to enjoy the highest level of restraint ...which is that in only you are in control... command yourself to hold back ... with great pleasure... not allowing a muscle to move... command your body to remain...still... so that there is no movement no reflex... give yourself that great pleasure of knowing that you are under complete control... and when you have done so ...and are ready to enjoy even more... look only into my eyes...

(test the subject with tickling, giving approval for her restraint)

Now allow yourself only to speak. Do you notice the pleasure you are creating? (wait) Good. I am going to reveal to you an equation for your enjoyment... Because there is an equation to enjoyment... first you feel the anticipation... then you participate fully... then you reflect back at a deep level on the enjoyment... Now you can do that at the deepest level of your inner mind... and as you do that you will **feel a connection with me**...*a connection that magnifies whatever pleasure I feel 100 times stronger for you... when I feel pleased you will automatically magnify your pleasure 100 times ... through the power of this connection... so imagine that connection now as a cord of light between you and me... and as i tell you "you have pleased me" feel*

Mind Control Hypnosis

that pleasure 100 more powerfully than me...don't you? (wait) That pleases me... that pleases me very much... and you have pleased me... to have learned so well... and to be so willing to learn in this manner... and it would please me that you learn more ... would you like to learn more? (wait)

[Emo chamber for reframing s&m with drills -> for org -> feeling shock only reminds your unconscious mind of the pleasure that you have control of]
You can learn now to turn anything into pleasure... if I strike the skin you can turn that shock into a ...release... of pleasure... and to do that first you must feel an anticipation... knowing that at some moment that shock will release all the pleasant feelings... but you will still have to wait... and let that anticipation build... can you **feel that anticipation?** (wait) ...let it build even more... powerfully ...as each second passes... so will the release build...

(proceed with spanking being VERY careful not to bruise or injure)
...and perhaps throughout the days to come you will feel the reminders of this on your skin and body... not know what they are or where they came from...forgotten to you conscious mind... only knowing that you enjoy the pleasure of learning...you enjoy the pleasure of learning...is this true?(wait)

[Yes set repeated -> do you have your new name? (get name) will be used only when doing these processes]

Mind Control Hypnosis

  Good ...now ... **go deeper...** and allow your self to respond completely to what you are learning to enjoy ... to my suggestions ...so that as you experience this pleasant state you can respond completely to my questions with a yes or no and each time go deeper... do you understand? (wait) Good.. so **go deeper** just as you will each time to you **respond this way to me**... now ....I want you... I deeply want you... to bring up the feeling of certainty... the certainty that you are learning and enjoying this process... bring up the feeling of certainty... and when you feel that certainty, with all your feelings say "yes" (wait)... and **go deeper...** now with that certainty bring forth the feeling of conviction... that what you are doing is right... bring up the that feeling of conviction and add it to your certainty and when you feel is ...with all your heart... say "yes" (wait) Good... now combine that with pleasure ... pleasure of know you are learning about control and freedom... powerful joyous pleasure and add that to your certainty and conviction and when you **feel that pleasure** say "yes"...Good. And you enjoy this don't you? (wait)... and enjoy responding so powerfully to each suggestion... don't you" (wait).

  There are many pleasures in life... emotional and physical pleasures.. there is the pleasure that is so... indulgent ...that you must have it... you want it ...it is that power pleasure of sexual pleasure...the wonderful powerful pleasure of sexual orgasm... and now on let that pleasure of orgasm build as you say "Yes" to accept each suggestion. (wait)

  That is right.... your mind is very powerful and you enjoy following my suggestions and commands. This is true isn't it? (wait)

Mind Control Hypnosis

[New Name will eagerly anticipate the next process]

When we started I told you that if you do well you will have a name...that you inner mind will give you... a name that you will instantly respond to ... day or night... awake or asleep... a name that will help you learn even more... that understanding has a strength a firmness that grows inside of you... wanting to do well ... and pleasing me so that you may choose your new name... and you have pleased me very much... So now your mind is under complete control and your inner mind can now reveal your new name.... What is the new name that your inner mind has chosen? (wait. For the purpose of the processes "New Name" will be used for the persons choice of name).

Very good. New Name, you have pleased me. You have pleased me very much, New Name. Will you agree to return again when I call you? (wait) Good! That pleases me!

So, New Name, I am now going to ask you to return to Names inner mind. Return ... hidden completely from her conscious awareness... locked away in right next to where she keeps everything that's true... so that you can secretly teach her how to enjoy life...and wait patiently for the next time you will will be called... by my voice and my voice only... this voice will call you... so that you can come forth and learn even more... and in those moments you can patiently restrain yourself... and guide her with your thoughts... and your strength... teaching her to enjoy life even more... and you will follow these suggestions and enjoy the power you

Mind Control Hypnosis

have in your restraint ... will you not?
Good. So go now. Go deeper... go deeper... forget... trust your inner mind to do it's perfect work.

[End Amnesia]

... and so you now know what it's like to have forgotten... your name completely... feeling just fine... and you can now retrieve your name, Name, and do you have it? Good... you've done wonderfully... and your inner mind will, Name, remember what it needs to forget or it may forget what you only think you remember... as it really doesn't even matter, it's not even important... you don't even have to think about it, Name, so just let it go...and even though it only took a brief minute of your time you'll emerge feeing absolutely wonderful... that's right, even though it only took a brief minute of time...you'll be amazed at how well you feel

*Now you will remember to remember that you can continue to learn you will discover new pleasures for yourself between now and when we next meet... that's right... new things will for you find new pleasures... in ways... that surprise and amaze you... to feel such joy and pleasure ... during the days and weeks to come... you'll find that you are enjoying life more in new ways and finding new ways to enjoy life... more fully ... and your inner mind creates an awareness that you are changing ... you are changing in all the ways **that you like** ... **that you enjoy**... you are changing in all the way you wanted to when you first heard my voice... and feels so natural ... it feels so easy... to make* these changes a part of you... that's right... new things will for you find new pleasures... in ways... that surprise and amaze you... to feel such joy and pleasure ... during the days and weeks to come...you will not touch yourself to enjoy that pleasure... you'll find that you are enjoying life more in new ways and finding new ways to enjoy life... more fully ... and your inner mind creates an awareness that you are changing ... you are changing in all the ways **that you like** ... **that you enjoy**... you are changing in all the ways you wanted to when you first heard our inner voice... speaking to you... and it feels so natural ... it feels so easy... to make these changes a part of you... do you agree to this? (wait for response) Good.

And even though all of this has taken just an instant you'll be amazed and surprised at how well you've done. That's right. Even this has been only a few brief **minute** you'll be pleasantly surprise at how well you've done.

And all of this is true

[give post hypnotic suggestion to laugh, enjoy life now upon awakening]

So allow yourself to return but only as quickly as you begin to smile and laugh ... for no apparent reason... Just bring yourself all the way back to the full awareness of the environment around you feeling wonderful laughing and smiling for all the reasons ... **that feels right**... for you.

There are additional scripts that are part of

Mind Control Hypnosis

the *Perfected Mind Control* process. They are quite explicit and can be used to further bind a subject to following orders. If you are serious about learning and applying them you can find them fully described in *Perfected Mind Control*, but be warned, they are not designed for those who have an irresponsible approach to power.

Mind Control Hypnosis

Conclusion

What I've tried to expose in this book have been some of the secrets used by hypnotists to overcome some of the most resistant hypnotic subjects. The end result is to assist them and to help them make the changes they want.

Possibly some of this information seemed intimidating and perhaps too powerful to be put in the hands of the unskilled masses. Perhaps it's true but my job is not to create and enforce some arbitrary hypnosis law. It is simply to inform.

Having read an early version of this book one of my friends had two responses. The first was how he would "zone out" when reading the hypnosis scripts. The second was a curious waxing that included creating a community of mind controlled hypnotic slaves. My response to him was 'Yes, it's possible but it is much likely to be more effort than it's worth."

To everyone else who reads this I ask that you put aside any juvenile fantasizes of power . It's very likely that when you finally have that power you will no longer need it.. Instead use it to make people happier and better.

So I end this book with the advise I gave at it's beginning.

Be fearless.

Dantalion Jones

Mind Control Hypnosis

Mind Control Language Patterns

by Dantalion Jones

Mind Control Language Patterns are phrases that can act as "triggers" to the people who hear them. They influence and control how we respond, and cause us to be influenced to do things without our knowing.

These language patterns are not fantasy, but are based on documented uses that come from psychology, hypnosis, Neuro Linguistic Programming, and studies of human behavior. *Mind Control Language Patterns* can be used to help and hurt. One can use *Mind Control Language Patterns* to create positive and lasting change in people, as well as feelings of trust, love and affection. They can also be used to induce amnesia, fear, insecurity and doubt. These types of patterns are what we call "dark" patterns. Knowing how to use these *Mind Control Language Patterns* gives you incredible power. Not knowing these *Mind Control Language Patterns* takes the control out of your hands, and places it into the hands of people who know their real power.

Available at Amazon.com or at

www.MindControlPublishing.com

Mind Control Hypnosis

Secrets Of Hypnotic Mind Control Report

By Marc Savage

After studying these programs for more than 11 years and over 1067 hours of reading, listening to audio programs and going to training classes, I realized they all lacked one big thing. A quick easy way to use these techniques NOW. Not after years of training and study.

    I have reviewed most, if not all of the courses you will find available. And they are all just fluff. They talk about hypnotic principles. They tell you about Milton Ericson who was considered to be the greatest hypnotist of all time. They talk about Richard Bandler the godfather of NLP.

    While this is all interesting and I will tell you I learned a lot they don't show you how to use these techniques. If you want a history lesson then these are the programs for you, but.

    If you want hard hitting easy, to use covert hypnotic mind control techniques then this is what you've been looking for.

Secrets Of Hypnotic Mind Control Report

By Marc Savage

www.secretsofmindcontrol.net

Mind Control Hypnosis

Hypnotherapy for 21st Century Healing & Success

"It is a great pleasure to have your book. Finding True Magic contains a great amount of practical information and creative guidance on the knowledge of mind and body derived from various disciplines of the Eastern and Western worlds." ~ Tulku Thondup, Tibetan Meditation Master, Author, The Healing Power of Mind

"East Meets West in *True Magic*. *Finding True Magic* is a remarkable textbook on Transpersonal Hypnotherapy. Recommended for deep study." ~ Ormand McGill, PhD., Dean of American Hypnotists

"Finding True Magic is a superb book. It's truly comprehensive and eclectic in its intelligent presentation of transpersonal work. It explores philosophy, metaphysics, eastern wisdom and their relationship to hypnotherapeutic healing. If you do healing work, you must have this book. If you teach, you and your students must have this book!" ~ Marilyn Gordon, CHT, Author, Extraordinary Healing

Purchase a signed copy of *Finding True Magic* and CD #1 for $50 – and save $7!

Go to www.FindingTrueMagic.com or send $50.00, check or money order (incl. S&H for US) to:

Jack Elias
Institute for Therapeutic Learning
P.O. Box 17229, Seattle, WA 98127

Phone: (206) 783-1838, jack@FindingTrueMagic.com

This book it utilized by teachers & students internationally for professional & personal growth.

Mind Control Hypnosis

Rich Mind, Poor Mind - Finding Emotional Freedom

by Jesse M. Berg

ISBN:1-60672-010-4

"Rich Mind, Poor Mind is a book that is exclusive in many ways. A unique writing style will intrigue you to continue and discover what is to be revealed next. You will find a combination of classic thinking about happiness mixed with a new approach of looking at the human condition."

"What if you could be shown the hiding place of the thieves of your peace of mind? You could use the spotlight of your awareness to cause these thieves to run for cover leaving you with a clear and quiet mind."

Available at Amazon.com or at

www.RichMindPoorMind.net

Mind Control Hypnosis

How to Hypnotized

The Complete Step-by-Step Guide to Stage Hypnosis

by Steve Hall

Simple step by step easy to follow guidance that reveals how to hypnotize people quickly and easily. Perfect for the absolute beginner with complete word for word scripts and practical demonstrations.

This is an ebook available for download at

www.InducingTrance.com

Readers say:

"I was just as shocked as my subject when I successfully hypnotized her within minutes. I didn't think it'd work and I'd be practicing for months!" ~ Daniel Stanton, UK.

"I successfully hypnotized my first subject using your book. He was hypnotized to a very deep trance and I was able to suggest he forgot his name and a number. It is a great feeling to achieve this!" ~ Richard Jackson, Norfolk, UK

Mind Control Hypnosis

Without Embarrassment: The Social Coward's Totally Fearless Seduction System

by Mike Pilinski

Without Embarrassment is by far the best book that you're going to find anywhere when it comes to addressing the single most important element of any man's romantic success -- those devilish misguided thoughts that go on deep inside your head where it relates to matters of the heart.

I'm especially talking about that galaxy of mojo-stealing ruminations and fears which are based upon deeply-seated internalized shame and self-hatred. These monsters can quietly begin to take over your consciousness until they eventually ruin entire aspects of your life.

"I am quite intelligent (169 IQ, 1510 SAT, MENSA member) and I must say that I found your book immensely enlightening and insightful much on the same scale that I found physics books such as Steven Hawking's A Brief History of Time, Feyman's Quantum ElectroDynamics and Lederman's The God Particle highly thought-provoking. I was humbled by your intellect and your knowledge of this material on a MASSIVE scale. You Sir are 'THE MAN.'"

~ Rick

www.HighStatusMale.com

Mind Control Hypnosis

The Persuasion Skills Black Book

by Rintu Basu

Acclaimed NLP trainer, Rintu Basu, has worked hard to devise this book so that you don't have to. As well as clearly laid-out chapters, examples and case studies, the whole book has been written using the very patterns you'll be learning. So, as you read and use your new skills, your conscious understanding and unconscious ability will continue to deepen.

These patterns are not necessarily about sending people into a hypnotic trance but just a way to move you from one perspective on an issue to another.

"I can get very excited when I think about the results people are likely to create using this material. If you spend a few minutes thinking about where, when and what results you are looking for I would guess you can get excited as well".

"In essence the little-known patterns and approaches I'm sharing can be used in all areas of your life to help you get more of what you want and less of what you don't."

Available at amazon.com or
www.thenlpcompany.com

Mind Control Hypnosis

Hands On Chaos Magic: Reality Manipulation Through the Ovayki Current

by Andrieh Vitimus

ISBN-10: 0738715085

Who said magical training had to be so dry and complicated? In this instructional text, Andrieh Vitimus banishes the severe tone of other esoteric orders and instead proposes a more accessible and practical approach - a course of study for the average Joe. From discovering new meditation positions through random dance to sculpting energy into playful balls, puppets, and form - fitting body suits, Vitimus' exercises are fun and irreverent while still imparting the skills needed for serious self-study."Hands-On Chaos Magic" emphasizes experimentation and finding out what works for you, and Vitimus makes it clear that pop magic is allowed. So you may want to try a spell from Harry Potter while assuming a Dragon Ball Z stance. Or maybe you'd like to bribe yourself into daily practice by 'kicking your mind's ass and then giving it candy'. By adopting a practical understanding of magical theory, readers will find magic easier to perform - and they'll achieve results more in line with their own notions of success.

Available at amazon.com

or

www.AndriehVitimus.com

Printed in Great Britain
by Amazon.co.uk, Ltd.,
Marston Gate.